101 Things To Do In

Las Vegas

Without Gambling

Compiled and edited by
Michael J Cullen

MYOL Books
2012

MYOL Books, Publisher
PO Box 80012
Raleigh NC 27623

Printed in the United States of America

Cover design by Tarrier Design

ISBN: 978-0-9845447-1-4

MYOL Books is an imprint of Quite Right Books, LLC

Contents

Introduction   7

Food and Drink

Hugo's Cellar	11
Top of the World	13
Samba Brazilian Steakhouse	15
Carnegie Deli	17
Max Brenner's	19
Sushi Roku	21
Wine Cellar and Tasting Room	23
Picasso	25
Circo	27
Mastro's Ocean Club	29
Jean Philippe Patisserie	31
Buffets	33
Dick's Last Resort	35
N9ne	37
Red Square	39
Burger Bar	41
Aureole	43
Border Grill	45
Joël Robuchon	47
Emeril's Fish House	49
Firefly*	51
Mon Ami Gabi	53
Carnival Court	55
Hash House a Go Go	57
Grand Lux Café	59
Delmonico Steakhouse	61
Lavo	63

Sightseeing

Bellagio Fountain Show	65
Bellagio Conservatory and Lobby	67
The Show in the Sky	69
Mirage Aquarium/Atrium	71
The Volcano	73
Sirens of TI	75
The Best View in Town	77
Million Dollar Photo Op	79
Flamingo Wildlife Habitat	81
Paris Las Vegas Sights	83
MGM Lion Habitat	85
Welcome to Las Vegas Sign	87

Shopping

Forum Shops	89
Grand Canal Shoppes	91
Fashion Show Mall	93
Bonanza Gifts	95

Activities

Fremont Street Experience	97
Madame Tussauds	99
The Auto Collections	101
Vegas Indoor Skydiving	103
Golf	105
Atomic Testing Museum	107
The Price is Right – Live	109
Nightclubs	111
Titanic: The Artifact Exhibition	113
Showcase Mall	115
The Gun Store	117
Day Spas	119
CSI: The Experience	121
Pinball Hall of Fame	123
Fast Lap Indoor Kart Racing	125
Helicopter Rides	127
Bellagio Gallery of Fine Art	129
Venetian Gondola Ride	131
Pools	133
CBS Television City Research Center	137
Exotics Racing School	139
Secret Garden and Dolphin Habitat	141
Gentlemen's Clubs	143
Bodies... The Exhibition	145
Stripper 101	147
Stratosphere Thrill Rides	149
Weddings	151
New York New York Roller Coaster	153
Gold and Silver Pawn	155
Dig This	157
Rent an Awesome Car	159
Neon Museum	161
Zero G	163
Shark Reef	165
Circus Circus/Adventuredome	167
Special Events	169

Shows

Mystére	173
Terry Fator	175
Celine Dion	177
Absinthe	179
Elton John	181
Penn and Teller	183
O	185
Jabbawockeez	187
Brad Garrett's Comedy Club	189
KÀ	191
The Amazing Jonathan	193
Barry Manilow	195
Jubilee!	197
Donny and Marie	199
Human Nature	201
Mac King Comedy Magic Show	203
Phantom – The Las Vegas Spectacular	205
Blue Man Group	207
Jersey Boys	209
Garth Brooks	211
Le Rêve	213
Tix 4 Tonight	215
Index	217

Introduction

Should You Read This Book?

During the compilation of this book, someone told us, "Las Vegas isn't for everyone." We had to think about that for a while. It felt wrong, but "everyone" includes a lot of people. Somewhere out there, you can probably find a person who doesn't enjoy shopping, or eating, or sightseeing, or partying, or going to shows, or golfing, or swimming, or clubbing, or thrill rides, or museums, or even a little taste of alcohol.

If that guy is out there, then Las Vegas and this book are probably not for him. For everyone else, there is a chance you will find something useful here.

Here are three types of people who will find this book valuable.

Person #1: Been There, Done Some of That — This person has been to Las Vegas one or more times. She knows it's a fun place, but she doesn't know about everything the city has to offer. This book will tell her about new places, and steer her towards some of the best ones.

Person #2: Never Been to Vegas, I Don't Gamble — Why wouldn't someone vacation in Las Vegas? The most common reason given is, "I don't gamble." Millions of people visit Las Vegas every year without gambling a dime. What are they doing, and why do they keep coming back? This book will tell you.

Person #3: The Experienced Vegas Visitor – This person has been to Las Vegas many times, and loves it. He wants to go back, but sometimes planning that next trip requires convincing Person #2 that it's a good idea. This is the book that you give to a friend, or a spouse, or a convention organizer at work, to convince them that Las Vegas is the best choice.

About the Selections in This Book

We chose the 101 Things in this book based upon the unscientific standard of "coolness." We're not saying that The Fonz would have enjoyed everything in the book, but if a guy can jump his motorcycle over a shark, he can probably appreciate a volcano that explodes every hour on the hour.

The chosen Things are not necessarily unique to Las Vegas, but you aren't likely to have one in your hometown. For instance, if this book had been published in the 1990s, we would have certainly included The Cheesecake Factory in the Caesars Palace Forum Shops. It wasn't the only one in the country, but Las Vegas was the only place many travelers could encounter one. Now they have over 150 locations, which pretty much makes them too widespread for inclusion in this book (though if you haven't been to a Cheesecake Factory, consider it Thing 102).

You'll notice that the reviews in this book are universally positive. We do not intend to give the impression that everything in Las Vegas is spotless and wonderful. There are thousands of restaurant and entertainment choices in town. Some of the shows are crummy. Some of the food places stink. They just aren't in this book. We chose 101 Things that we think are cool. If something sucks, it isn't in the book (okay, there is one exception).

It's worth mentioning a few words on matters of cost. In the selection of the 101 Things, price was not a major factor. Some of the coolest attractions are free, while others are ridiculously expensive. Overall, the city tends to be expensive, but fear not – discounts are available. Some are mentioned in this book, but others must be sought online. It's always worth visiting the website of any place you plan to visit. A Google search of the place name plus "coupon" or "discount" can save you some nice coin. On many of the Things, we supply a price or price range. Consider these prices no more than estimates, because...

Things change. This is true pretty much everywhere, but it is doubly true in Las Vegas. The competition for tourist dollars is brutal. Restaurants, clubs and attractions come and go at a lightning pace. Two of our 101 Things bit the dust during the compilation of this book, and had to be replaced. If you see some things you like, don't hesitate to go and try them out. We can't guarantee you'll have fun, but we like your odds.

Help Us Keep Up With the Changes

Shortly before we went to press, the Sahara Hotel and Casino closed, robbing us of their excellent Speed: The Ride roller coaster. The Liberace Museum also closed. Fortunately, we had plenty of cool choices to include in their places.

As Las Vegas changes, portions of this book will become outdated or incorrect. So we're asking you to help us keep up with this rapidly changing city.

If you find something in the book that is, in your experience, incorrect, just drop us a note at:

vegas101@nc.rr.com

We'll be using your advice, and our own experiences, to keep each edition of the book as up-to-date as possible.

Also, if you find something new and cool that screams for inclusion in the book, just let us know.

Thanks,

Michael J Cullen, Editor

Hugo's Cellar

If you're looking for that classy, old school Las Vegas vibe, you can't do better than dinner at Hugo's Cellar. Located downstairs (as you probably guessed) beneath the Four Queens resort and casino, the folks in the Cellar are pretty straightforward about their offering. You're going to choose from a menu that has barely changed in decades because there was never a need. You'll get quality cuts of meat, fresh seafood, and extraordinarily friendly service.

The nice touches begin as soon as you walk through the door. Each lady in your party will be presented with a single red rose. Is that corny? Maybe, but you're not likely to see anyone handing it back.

After you order, your waiter will return at the helm of a large salad cart. He will then proceed to use the cart's extensive selection to build you a salad, item by item. No egg. Yes pine nuts. No anchovies. Yes shrimp. Whatever you like. The result is the salad of your dreams, assuming you're a person who dreams of salads.

When your entree arrives, it will probably not look like a piece of avant-garde art from a celebrity chef. It will look like food. Your veal chop, lobster or Beef Wellington will look pretty much as you expect. They will also taste pretty much as you expect, assuming you expect them to taste pretty darn good.

The dessert highlights are the Bananas Foster or the cherries jubilee, either of which they will flambé at your table.

The last nice touch is a tray of chocolate-dipped fruits with cream. Like the salad, it's included in your entree price.

Entrees at Hugo's Cellar range from $35 to $52. That price becomes a bit more reasonable when you consider that the salad and the chocolate fruits are included. Make a reservation because they can be quite busy, and you don't want to get caught downtown without a dinner plan.

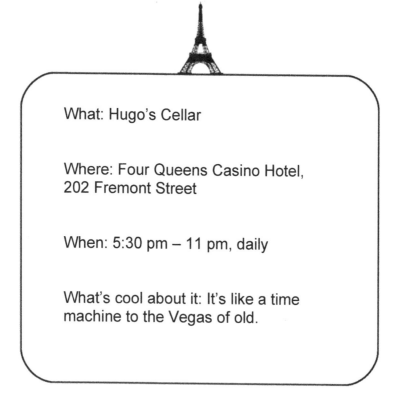

What: Hugo's Cellar

Where: Four Queens Casino Hotel, 202 Fremont Street

When: 5:30 pm – 11 pm, daily

What's cool about it: It's like a time machine to the Vegas of old.

Top of the World

Imagine enjoying an excellent dinner 844 feet above the ground, in a restaurant that slowly rotates to give you a panoramic view of the coolest city in the world. If you're good at following instructions, you just imagined yourself at Top of the World, the Stratosphere hotel and casino's contribution to Las Vegas fine dining.

Your journey will begin on the second floor. After identifying yourself as someone with a reservation, you will be guided to an elevator that will whisk you up to the 108th floor. Your ears will pop. It helps to swallow.

If you're a little early, hop on down to the Level 107 lounge and grab a drink. It doesn't rotate, but it offers the same stratospheric view as the restaurant. The lounge has live music most nights after 6 pm.

You will soon be led to your table in the rotating dining room. Don't worry. It's not a CD player; it's a restaurant. The rotation is quite slow. It takes 80 minutes for the full 360 degree ride, so you'll have ample opportunity to see all of the city and beyond. The experience is especially poignant near the end of your trip, offering a different perspective as you look down upon the various places you have visited.

The food is inevitably fated to be overshadowed by the view. That said, the choices are excellent. The lobster bisque is a standout. The steaks surpass many of the more celebrated steakhouses in town. Most items are available a la carte, but there is usually a tasting menu available. There's even a three-course vegan tasting menu.

Most wine drinkers find the selection more than adequate. Wine Spectator clearly thinks so, since they have given their Award of Excellence to Top of the World each year since 1996.

If you leave room for dessert, the cheesecake lollipops are ridiculous.

Dinner entrees at Top of the World range from $40-$65. They are open daily for lunch, and you can save significantly that way.

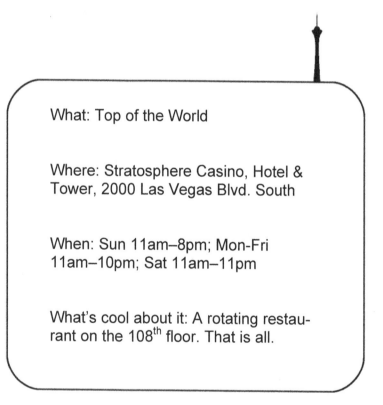

What: Top of the World

Where: Stratosphere Casino, Hotel & Tower, 2000 Las Vegas Blvd. South

When: Sun 11am–8pm; Mon-Fri 11am–10pm; Sat 11am–11pm

What's cool about it: A rotating restaurant on the 108th floor. That is all.

Samba Brazilian Steakhouse

What's the best advice for visitors to Samba Brazilian Steakhouse in The Mirage? Come hungry. The menu features some delicious appetizers and excellent entrees, but the highlight of a trip to Samba is the Rodizio. For those unfamiliar with the Brazilian steakhouse concept, here it is. For a flat price, you are provided with a selection of traditional Brazilian side dishes. You can expect black beans and rice, plantains, creamed spinach, farofa carrots, and a bottomless bowl of "Samba Salad" that is tossed tableside. You are also provided with a wooden marker that is painted red on one side and green on the other. You begin with the red side facing upwards.

After a few minutes spent tasting the side dishes, you can turn you marker green side up. This is the signal for the action to begin. Soon, a man carrying a long skewer and a sharp knife will approach you. It's okay. He is friendly. He brings you meat. The meat has been slow-roasting in the kitchen, and the man will cut you off a piece or two, if that's what you like. Other men will follow, exhibiting the same generous behavior, but with a variety of different meats. This will continue until you turn your marker back to the red side, signaling the servers that the meat service should pause. Don't worry, you can turn it back to green any time you want.

The meat choices are numerous and varied. There's a "Picanha" style sirloin, a ginger style flank steak, slow cooked sausage and sweet peppers, as well as daily lamb and pork selections. Bird lovers might enjoy the "Ahlo" style chicken legs, the Huli Huli chicken Hawaiian style, or the honey brushed turkey breast roulade wrapped in bacon. The individual meats can change over time, but the variety is always fantastic.

The Rodizio at Samba is all-you-can-eat for a flat price of $39.95 per person. The a la carte entrees could save you a little money. They come with the same great sides, but they won't leave you with that warm feeling of carnivorous excess.

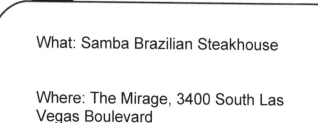

What: Samba Brazilian Steakhouse

Where: The Mirage, 3400 South Las Vegas Boulevard

When: 5:00 pm – 10:30 pm

What's cool about it: A parade of men bringing large slabs of meat to your table.

Carnegie Deli

The Carnegie Deli has been a Manhattan fixture since 1937. The Las Vegas version of the storied eatery can be found inside The Mirage, serving kosher and non-kosher delights to hungry tourists.

Any discussion of the Carnegie Deli has to begin with their sandwiches. The rumors are true. The sandwiches are stacked ridiculously, monstrously high with meat. If you order the pastrami or corned beef, it's likely to contain over a pound of meat. Seriously, it's going to look like a skyscraper on your plate. Not all of the meals are that extreme, but the portions are pretty strong across the board. Their unofficial motto is, "If you can finish your meal, we've done something wrong."

When it comes to ingredients, they do something right. In order to ensure consistent quality, they cure, pickle and smoke their own meats.

If you're not looking for a leaning tower of lunchmeat, the Milton's Smorgasbord is a standout. It features four freshly-baked rolls topped with shrimp salad, tuna salad, egg salad and chicken salad. It's enough to feed two people, or one very hungry person. You decide. Then again, that's pretty much the choice you make on many of the items.

For most people, "sandwich place" equals "lunch place," but the Carnegie Deli is open 24 hours a day. If you need a nosh at 3 a.m., they're there for you. In fact, if you crave breakfast at 3 a.m., they're still there for you, with a sizable breakfast menu that's served all day and all night. You might be able to find a better cheese blintz somewhere else in Las Vegas, but good luck searching.

The giant portions here will probably put your tab in the $20-$25 range per person. Many of the larger items are sharable, and even with the $3 sharing charge, you can come out way ahead.

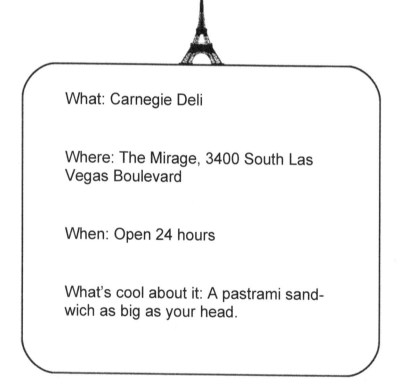

What: Carnegie Deli

Where: The Mirage, 3400 South Las Vegas Boulevard

When: Open 24 hours

What's cool about it: A pastrami sandwich as big as your head.

Max Brenner, Chocolate by the Bald Man

Max Brenner has opened a shrine to chocolate in the Caesars Palace Forum Shops. You might as well plan on going there, because the sweet smell of chocolate is going to pull you in.

In spite of the alluring aroma, not everything here is dessert. There's a sizable and tasty menu to be tackled first. The slider bar features traditional burger-style sliders, plus a handful of unusual choices, like the Crispy Chicken Slider "Cobb Style," with avocado, bacon and bleu cheese. In addition to the pizza, salad and burger choices, there are some well done pasta dishes and dinner crepes. If you literally can't wait for the chocolate, try the waffle fries. They are covered in a light dusting of chili powder and cocoa powder.

It's easy to make the rookie mistake of filling up on the excellent entrees. The portions are generous. If you manage to dodge this hurdle, then it's time for the main event – dessert.

Let's get one thing straight. This place is about chocolate. There aren't "some" chocolate desserts or "a lot of" chocolate desserts. All of the desserts contain chocolate. You might be able to wangle a fruit smoothie off of the drink menu, but dessert at Max Brenner's means chocolate.

All of the desserts are pleasingly presented, with a reverence for chocolate in mind. There are chocolate waffles, crepes, cookies and pizzas. There are chocolate cakes, shakes, fondues and eggrolls. There's the Euphoria Peanut Butter Chocolate Fudge Sundae, which stands as high as an elephant's eye. Its massive sundae glass is packed with two kinds of ice cream, caramelized toffee bananas, pure chocolate chunks, warm chocolate and peanut butter sauce, and crunchy hazelnut bits. Finishing it is not a job for one.

Everything is served in distinctive Max Brenner accessories. Your shake arrives in an Alice Cup, with the words "Drink Me" printed on the side. Hot chocolate is served in an oblong Hug Mug, designed to be cradled in two hands. Both items, and many more, are available in the sizable gift shop.

What: Max Brenner, Chocolate by the Bald Man

Where: The Forum Shops at Caesars, 3500 Las Vegas Boulevard South

When: Sun-Thur 10 am-11 pm, Fri-Sat 10 am-12 am

What's cool about it: So much chocolate. it's even on the waffle fries.

Sushi Roku

For a taste of some of the best sushi in town, make your way to Sushi Roku, in the Caesars Palace Forum Shops. Their modern Japanese cuisine is served in a tasteful, minimalist Zen environment, by a friendly and attentive staff. They also boast one of the most fantastic views of the central Strip you can find, especially at night. You can see the neon lights of Paris, Bally's, Planet Hollywood and more, all from the comfort of your booth.

There's a full sushi menu to choose from, but the Chef's Sashimi Combination is a good place to start. If you're looking for something that isn't on the menu, the expert sushi chefs are more than willing to concoct something from the fresh ingredients at hand. They also make their own wasabi, and you can tell. The freshly-ground roots pack an extra punch.

The dinner menu features steaks, chicken, fish and tempura. If you're looking for actual Japanese kobe beef, sorry, you won't find it here. The American "Kobe" New York Steak will still melt in your mouth.

Also worthwhile is the Chef's Omakase tasting menu, with a representative sample of the best the restaurant has to offer. Sushi. Sashimi. The works.

Are you in the mood for some sake? Order a bottle from their list of over two dozen selections. A tasting sampler of three sakes is also available.

Sushi Roku is not a place to find bargain basement sushi. The sushi runs $3-6 per piece, and the rolls are $8 and up. Entrees range from $24 to $55. The Omakase fixed menu is $90 per person.

When you make your reservation, ask for a booth with a view of The Strip. It's never a guarantee, but it greatly increases your chance of getting the dynamite view.

What: Sushi Roku

Where: The Forum Shops at Caesars, 3500 Las Vegas Boulevard South

When: Sun-Thur 12 pm-10 pm, Fri-Sat 12 pm-11 pm

What's cool about it: Homemade wasabi that's eye-wateringly good.

The Wine Cellar and Tasting Room

Inside the Rio Hotel and Casino, there's a place called the Masquerade Village. It's a loud place, ringing with the sounds of music, slot machines, and what can pretty much be described as a non-stop party. If you take the not very well marked staircase to the Wine Cellar and Tasting Room, you will find an oasis of calmness just a few feet beneath the craziness of the casino.

The Wine Cellar and Tasting Room is both of the things its name implies, and much more. It is part bar, part wine shop, part museum, and a large part relaxation destination.

When you get to the bottom of those stairs, you will realize that you're in an actual wine cellar "decorated" by over 50,000 bottles. Many of them are rare and available for sale. Some are just for gawking, like the bottle of 1800 Madeira from Thomas Jefferson's cellar, or the vertical collection of Chateau d'Yquem (with a bottle from each of the years from 1855-1990).

When it comes time for you to enjoy some of the wine, you can do so at the bar, at a table, or on one of the cushy leather couches. Over 100 wines are available by the glass, and many are served in tasting flights. If you're looking for something to nibble, a number of freshly baked breads and excellent cheeses are available. Your server can recommend a cheese flight appropriate to the wines you have chosen.

Overall, the staff has knowledge and they're willing to share. It doesn't matter if you're just looking to unwind and enjoy a glass, or if you're a seasoned wine snob, the people here can speak your language.

Expect to pay around $15-$25 per person for this detour, but they can certainly accommodate you if your tastes run towards the rare or expensive.

What: The Wine Cellar & Tasting Room

Where: Rio Suites Hotel and Casino, 3700 West Flamingo Road

When: Mon & Thur 4 pm-10pm, Fri & Sat 3 pm-11 pm, Sun 3 pm-10 pm

What's cool about it: Some rare peace and quiet, 10 feet beneath a casino.

Picasso

The Picasso restaurant inside the Bellagio has the feel of a place the artist himself would have enjoyed. The dining room is a mixture of colors, bright and warm. The room is decorated with handiworks, from the humble, yet whimsical, collection of clay pots that hang from the ceiling near the entrance, to the fabulous Picasso paintings that grace the walls. The eleven Picassos have an estimated value of $50 million, but they are yours to enjoy for the duration of your meal.

That meal will be a creation of award-winning Chef Julian Serrano, who, unlike many executive chefs in town, can be found in the kitchen most nights. His French cuisine comes with a Spanish flair. The menu changes regularly, at the whim of the chef, but you are likely to find Serrano's U-10 Day Boat Scallops and his famous foie gras. Each course is designed to be enjoyed visually, frequently incorporating the colorful patterns of the Picasso fine china.

Oenophiles will find much to admire in the enormous Picasso wine list. Master Sommelier Robert Smith captains a collection of over 1500 selections. He and his staff are generous with their time, offering all the information you need to make the wine choice that suits you best.

Another feature of many of the fine dining restaurants inside the Bellagio is an opportunity to view the wonderful Bellagio Fountain Show. Most tables in Picasso will afford you a view of the dancing waters, but if you are willing to forego the company of the paintings, ask for a table on the terrace, and enjoy what is possibly the finest view of the fountains there is.

Picasso provides a couple of fixed menus at a cost of $113-$123 per person. Wine pairings for each course are available for $53-$63 per person.

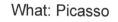

What: Picasso

Where: Bellagio, 3600 Las Vegas Boulevard South

When: Wed-Mon 5:30 pm-9:30 pm

What's cool about it: $50 million worth of masterpieces in your dining room.

Circo

It's hard to find a spot in the Bellagio that isn't a feast for the eyes. Circo is no exception. The circus-themed décor is fun, yet elegant. The view of Lake Bellagio is pleasing at any time, but especially satisfying when the superb Bellagio Fountain Show is playing. One way to improve upon a spectacular view is to enjoy it alongside a gourmet meal. The folks at Circo can help you out with that.

Based upon the renowned Manhattan eatery of the same name (and with the same owners), Circo offers upscale Tuscan cuisine. The pastas are handmade. The ravioli with sheep's milk ricotta is a favorite. You can't go wrong with any of the thin crust pizzas. The menu changes seasonally, but you can always count on a wide selection of meats and seafood. The pistachio crusted Maine lobster is another winner.

The wine selection is excellent, with over 900 bottles offered. There is a definite focus on Italian wines, but the selection from other countries is good.

Circo can be seen as an affordable alternative to its sister restaurant Le Cirque, the extraordinary French eatery next door. Without that comparison you're unlikely to describe it as inexpensive. Entrees range from $20-$50, but with soup, salad, appetizer and wine you can easily approach a $200 dinner for two. A three-course prix fixe meal can often be had for under $60 per person, which makes it a relative bargain.

The Bellagio is the home to one of the best shows in town, Cirque du Soleil's "O". They frequently have dinner and show packages available through their website (for Circo and other restaurants). If you have tickets to see "O", mention it to the wait staff. Your server will pace the service to make sure you get to the show on time.

What: Circo

Where: Bellagio, 3600 Las Vegas Boulevard South

When: 5:30 pm-10:30 pm, daily

What's cool about it: A front row seat for the Bellagio Fountain Show.

Mastro's Ocean Club

Diners in southern California and Arizona already know that the Mastro's name is synonymous with great steaks. Visitors to Crystals in City Center can now experience the Mastro's magic for themselves. Fish fans will want to begin with their famous Seafood Tower. A variety of oysters, crab, prawns, and whatever else you want to add, are packed in ice and presented in a chilled tower. You can add pieces of fresh seafood to customize the tower to the size of your group. When they need more room, they just add another level. Bits of dry ice make the spectacle even more impressive.

The entrees are comprised of melt-in-your-mouth steaks and excellent seafood choices. The Bone-in Filet and the Chilean Sea Bass stand at the head of a very impressive class.

The sizable side dishes can be shared by at least two people. Everyone talks about the Lobster Mashed Potatoes, and rightly so. If you were expecting tiny bits of lobster in your side dish, you will be pleasantly surprised these large, delectable chunks. The Gorgonzola Mac & Cheese might be the best mac & cheese that you've ever had.

If you've managed to leave room for dessert, remember where you are. You can get a good Crème Brûlée at various places around town, but this is the only place you can enjoy Mastro's Signature Warm Butter Cake. Don't let this opportunity pass.

If you've ever been inside the Crystals mall at City Center, there's no way you could have missed the 80-

foot tall sculptural Tree House. What is it? It's art, and it's a dining room. Who are those people inside it? Those are Mastro's customers enjoying some really good food. If you like the idea of dining inside a giant work of art, mention it when you make your reservation. They can usually get you a spot. There's also another dining room with live piano music, if you'd rather not be the center of attention.

Dinner at Mastro's is at the high end of the price scale, even for Las Vegas. Expect to pay $100 per person, plus the cost of alcohol.

What: Mastro's Ocean Club

Where: Crystals at CityCenter, 3720 Las Vegas Boulevard South

When: Sun-Thur 5 pm-11 pm, Fri-Sat 5 pm-12 am

What's cool about it: Fine dining inside an 80-foot treehouse.

Jean Philippe Patisserie

World champion pastry chef Jean-Philippe Maury has Las Vegas figured out. Both of his Jean Philippe Patisserie locations combine delectable treats with eye-popping sights to deliver an experience you'll find nowhere else.

The Bellagio location isn't very large, but it packs a lot into a small space. Early in the day you can find croissants and delicious pastries. A selection of sandwiches appears at lunch time. There's a crepe station, where a chef will make you a personalized crepe with sweet or savory fillings of your choice. If you're a fan of gelato, you'll find a large selection of flavors. All of them are made on-site.

The culinary highlight has to be the selection of dessert pastries. Each one is hand crafted by a pastry chef, and each pastry is its own work of art. When they are laid out in rows, it's almost as if they combine to form a large, edible interactive sculpture.

There's a lot of chocolate here, too. While you might grab a box of Jean Philippe chocolates to take with you, that box will probably not contain your most vivid chocolate memory from this trip. The one thing everyone remembers about Jean Philippe Patisserie is the fountain.

Melted chocolate pours from the ceiling in streams of white, milk, and dark. The three streams cascade over a series of glass leaves, creating the world's largest chocolate fountain (Guinness says so!). A glass wall prevents you from sticking your mouth into the stream and opening wide, but you know you want to.

A second location is located near the guest elevators at the Aria. It lacks the chocolate fountain, but in every other way the Aria location screams "bigger" and "more." While the original location is small, this one sprawls, with plenty of seating. The place is visually stunning, decorated in black and white, glass and chrome.

Everything from the original location can be found here too – and then some. There's a huge case of chocolates that you can purchase by the piece, and a far larger selection of packaged merchandise to bring home.

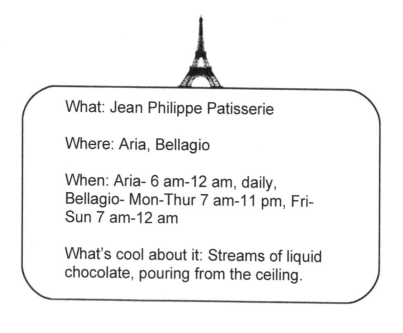

What: Jean Philippe Patisserie

Where: Aria, Bellagio

When: Aria- 6 am-12 am, daily, Bellagio- Mon-Thur 7 am-11 pm, Fri-Sun 7 am-12 am

What's cool about it: Streams of liquid chocolate, pouring from the ceiling.

Buffets

Las Vegas is known for its selection of all you can eat buffets. Virtually every resort offers its own version of fixed-price smorgasbord. The buffets in Vegas are an excellent example of getting what you pay for. Those with the best food tend to charge the most money. You can still find the occasional bargain buffet, but you have to ask yourself – did you travel all the way to Las Vegas to eat at a Golden Corral? If not, some of these buffets might be to your liking.

The Buffet – Wynn Las Vegas

This is the buffet of a five diamond resort. You expect quality and they deliver. The dining room is beautiful. The servers are attentive. The chefs at the live cooking stations prepare it the way you want it. The prime rib and smoked salmon are rightfully popular. Save room for dessert from the crepe station or the nice gelato selection.

The Buffet – Bellagio

The same superlatives that described the Wynn Buffet can be applied to the Bellagio's offering. The two are pretty much neck and neck for best buffet in town. Expect a large seafood selection. The swordfish is a standout. The common buffet strategy of not filling up on side dishes can backfire here, causing you to miss a superior mac and cheese, and some unique pesto mashed potatoes.

Spice Market Buffet – Planet Hollywood

When Planet Hollywood bought the Aladdin resort, they systematically eliminated the various pieces of the Arabian theme. The Spice Market Buffet remains. It was too good to replace. The selection and quality of the Asian and Middle Eastern foods sets them apart from other places. Dessert crepes are always a nice way to finish a meal.

Studio B – M Resort

The M Resort is a few miles south of The Strip, but the Studio B Buffet makes the trip worthwhile. Their selection is as large as any buffet in town. It also features a show kitchen, with live cooking demonstrations. The cost is noticeably less than the other buffets on this list. Beer and wine is included in your price, which makes an excellent deal even better.

Wicked Spoon Buffet – Cosmopolitan

The Wicked Spoon features the prettiest dining area of all the Vegas buffets, and easily the most pleasing food presentation. Each item comes presented on its own plate, or in its own little metal pot, or in its own little basket. The effect is both cute and classy. None of those things would be important if the food wasn't good, but don't worry, it is.

Dick's Last Resort

Dick's Last Resort is one of those places that you shouldn't just wander into blindly. Anyone expecting the courteous service that is the norm in Las Vegas eateries would be in for quite a shock. Dick's calls itself "The Shame o' The Strip" for a good reason, and the shame begins with the service.

Your waiter might insult you. Or yell at you. Or ignore you. Or throw food at you. Or call you by a nasty nickname. Or flip you the bird. Or put a paper hat on your head that makes fun of your penis size. Even if you're a girl.

The abuse is part of the fun. It isn't the kind of thing you would want going on during a romantic dinner for two, but it can be hilarious for a group looking for a rambunctious good time. If loud music, frequent laughter, and a large bartender named Taco (according to the tattoo on his belly) sound like fun to you, then this is probably your kind of place.

The menu reflects the overall crude attitude. What would you drink to wash down their Big Ass Burger? If you guessed a Big Ass Beer, you'd be correct. Be careful, or you might end up with a Case o' Snow Crabs. And there is just no apologizing for the Pork Bonerz. Silly names aside, what you're really getting is glorified bar food. It's tasty bar food, but you will not confuse it with gourmet fare.

Dick's Last Resort is located in the Excalibur hotel/casino. Most of the entrees are in the $11-$17 range, so it's a bit pricy for what you get. Consider it a surcharge for the unapologetically vulgar environment. Kids are welcome, but as parents, you'll have to decide whether or not it's a great idea. They might hear a few words you haven't taught them yet.

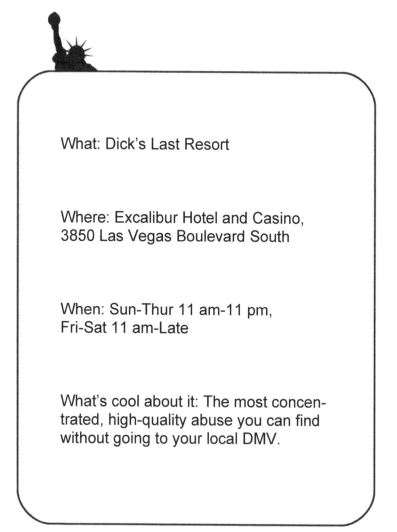

What: Dick's Last Resort

Where: Excalibur Hotel and Casino, 3850 Las Vegas Boulevard South

When: Sun-Thur 11 am-11 pm, Fri-Sat 11 am-Late

What's cool about it: The most concentrated, high-quality abuse you can find without going to your local DMV.

N9ne Steakhouse

Plenty of Las Vegas restaurants can offer an upscale dining experience, but none of them offer the combination of food, service and trendiness you can find at N9ne Steakhouse (save your sanity, and pronounce it "nine").

There is no guarantee that you're going to see a celebrity at N9ne. Celebrities blow into and out of Las Vegas like the very considerable wind. You never know when or where, but there will be some. That said, N9ne offers the best chance of spotting the rich/famous in a restaurant setting.

It's easy to be dazzled by the swank furnishings, the stunning champagne and caviar bar, and the 300-color intelligent lighting system that controls the mood. The bottom line is this: it's still a restaurant. Celebrities wouldn't be coming here if the food wasn't good.

One of N9ne's founders is the son of Arnie Morton, the restaurateur who brought us Morton's Steakhouse of Chicago, so it shouldn't be surprising that they know how to cook a steak. The prime aged meat is broiled in a 1200 degrees oven in order to retain its natural juiciness. All of the traditional cuts are available, but the 40 oz. bone-in ribeye deserves special attention. The meal is designed for two, but the occasional maniac has tried his luck solo.

The non-steak menu is primarily devoted to seafood. The Tuna Steak Diane and the Organic Scottish Salmon are highlights. Also, all of their steaks "surf," so you can create your own surf and turf by adding lobster,

Alaskan king crab legs or baked stuffed jumbo shrimp to your beef. The seafood equivalent to the giant ribeye is the 1 ½ pound coldwater lobster tail that looks like it came off of a sea monster. The N9ne Steakhouse is located in the Palms hotel/casino. Entrees and steaks range from $25-59 per person. Appetizers and sides will push the bill higher. The ginormous lobster tail breaks the price structure totally.

What: N9ne Steakhouse

Where: Rio Suites Hotel and Casino, 3700 West Flamingo Road

When: Sun-Thur 5 pm-10 pm, Fri-Sat 5 pm-11 pm

What's cool about it: Beautiful steaks and beautiful people

Red Square

If you go to Red Square in the Mandalay Bay hotel and casino, and you find the Imperial Russian/Soviet décor to be a bit off-putting, think of it this way. The United States won the cold war, and we got a pretty neat restaurant out of the deal. Oh, and a lot of vodka.

The relentless theme begins before you enter the restaurant, when you are faced with a giant statue of Vladimir Lenin at the front door. The statue lacks Lenin's head, but it makes up for it by being covered in an amazing amount of (hopefully) fake pigeon poop. The interior is decorated with bits of Russia's past. Flags. Posters. Newspapers. Whatever ya got.

When it comes to the food, you're in luck. Many of the items have Russian names, but thankfully, they do not taste like they were made in Russia. The Siberian Nachos are not actually Siberian, but they are a tasty mix of wonton chips, smoked salmon and wasabi. Red Square boasts the best caviar menu on The Strip. Many of the caviars are from Russia, but that's okay. It's caviar.

The restaurant serves quality food, but the bar is the main attraction. Their massive vodka selection tops 200 choices from over two dozen countries. A variety of vodka tasting menus allow you to compare and contrast the world's finest.

They will infuse your vodka with interesting flavors. They will mix your vodka into wonderful drinks. The best way to appreciate the various vodkas, though, is straight. And cold. The bar is covered in ice, to make sure none of your selections approach room temperature. There is an even colder option, though.

When you purchase a bottle of vodka, you and your party get to enter the vodka vault. This sub-zero room will allow you to enjoy your choice in its intended environment. Complimentary fur coats and hats are provided for your stay. And no, you aren't drunk. That's Lenin's head in the vault.

What: Red Square

Where: Mandalay Bay Resort and Casino, 3950 Las Vegas Blvd. South

When: Sun-Thur 4 pm-1 am, Fri-Sat 4 pm-2 am

What's cool about it: A vodka freezer that requires winter clothing.

Burger Bar

For many years the Burger King motto has been "Have it your way." It was their way of letting you know that you don't have to have onions on your Whopper. They can take them off if you like. It may not sound like much, but it was a small step forward in burger evolution.

If Burger King was a small step, then celebrity chef Hubert Keller's Burger Bar is a giant leap. You're not going to see something like the Surf and Turf Burger (black angus beef, grilled half lobster, grilled green asparagus) at Burger King, and it will be a long time before you can walk into McDonald's and find The Rossini (kobe beef, sautéed foie gras, shaved truffles).

If the whole "chef thing" sounds a bit too fancy for a burger place, that's no problem. You can craft your own burger from an extensive ingredient list.

You start by choosing the meat from various types of beef, including buffalo. If beef isn't your thing, you can choose the turkey or veggie option. You can also select from five different types of bun.

Then the fun really begins. Burger Bar features an a la carte menu of over three dozen burger toppings. The list includes pretty much everything you've ever dreamed of putting on a hamburger, and quite a few things you haven't. Why just settle for one type of cheese when you can have eight? Want bacon? You're going to have to be more specific, since there are four different types on the menu. Want smoked salmon on your burger? Marinated anchovies? Cranberry sauce? A fried egg? You'll probably want to spend a little extra time with the menu, creating our own, personalized Franken-burger.

Many Las Vegas restaurants have world class wine lists, but wine is a bit stuffy for a burger place. Burger Bar has a world class beer list. With two dozen beers on tap and over 100 bottled selections, even the most jaded beer aficionado is likely to find something new.

Bring your appetite, especially if you want one of the dessert "burgers" that come served on a warm donut.

Burger Bar is located in Mandalay Place, adjacent to the Mandalay Bay resort. Reservations are not re-quired, but they're a good idea.

What: Burger Bar

Where: Mandalay Bay Resort and Casino, 3950 Las Vegas Boulevard South

When: Sun-Thur 11 am-11 pm, Fri-Sat 11 am-1 am

What's cool about it: Over one trillion burger and beer combinations

Aureole

The first thing you notice when you walk into Aureole is the gigantic tower of wine, which may or may not have young women flying around it. The glass and steel tower is 42-feet tall, and is the largest in the world. It houses 10,000 bottles of the restaurant's enormous collection. Another 50,000 bottles are in the cellar. If you order a bottle from the tower it will be retrieved by a "wine angel." The spandex-clad angels navigate the tower with the aid of remote-controlled harnesses and pulleys. They take pride in retrieving your bottle in three minutes or less.

Even the act of ordering a bottle of wine is different here. The wine list can be found on the notebook computer provided by your wait staff. Search it, sort it, and choose the bottle you like. You can even consult their online wine list and reserve your choice before you arrive.

Top chef Charlie Palmer believes that "people eat with their eyes long before they put fork to food," so the Progressive American Cuisine dishes at Aureole are culinary works of art. Most people choose one of the innovative prix-fixe menus, but a la carte selections are available as well. A parallel tasting menu matches an appropriate wine to each course.

The main dining room is large, and can feel very busy. For a more romantic experience, request the Swan Court. This intimate room has only 14 tables and offers a peaceful view of a small waterfall and a pond with live swans. Only the multi-course prix fixe menus are available in Swan Court, and a small ($10) premium is added to the menus served there.

Aureole is located in the Mandalay Bay resort. Most of the prix fixe menus range from $55-95 per person. The wine can make a dent in your wallet as well, especially if you're the type to enjoy the occasional $10,000 bottle.

What: Aureole

Where: Mandalay Bay Resort and Casino, 3950 Las Vegas Blvd. South

When: 5:30 pm-12 am, nightly

What's cool about it: Women in spandex who fly through the air and bring you wine. What a country.

Border Grill

Viewers of the Food Network are familiar with Chefs Mary Sue Milliken and Susan Feniger, the hosts of the popular "Too Hot Tamales." If you think their food looks good on TV, you owe it to yourself to visit their Border Grill in Mandalay Bay.

The two-story restaurant is bright and appealing. You can choose indoor seating or a table on the outdoor patio, overlooking the Mandalay beach and the lazy river.

The cuisine is upscale Mexican, featuring a variety of familiar dishes with colorful and unusual twists. The Plantain Empanadas are always a nice way to start things off. The taco choices include fish (beer battered or grilled), Yucatan pork, or Kobe beef. Their version of the Chili Relleno is one of the best you'll find anywhere. A gluten-free menu is also available.

If you want a drink with your meal, or maybe just want to enjoy a cocktail on the patio, don't worry. There is alcohol. In addition to a nice selection of wines and beers, there's a serious list of interesting margaritas and specialty drinks. The Border Bloody Mary uses home-made, chile infused vodka that packs a nice punch.

On the weekend they serve an extraordinary brunch. The brunch items are served on small plates, but your server will gladly bring you as many as you want. Some of the items are from the regular menu, but many are just for the brunch. If you're looking for a breakfast combination you've never had before, try the

Guava Empanada, the Coconut French Toast, or the Chorizo and Egg Taco.

Border Grill is open for both lunch and dinner. Lunch entrees tend to range from $16-$24. Dinner entrees go from $21-$36. A three-course dinner is available for $42, which is a pretty nice deal. The all you can eat brunch is $24.99, plus $5, if you want the free flowing Mimosas.

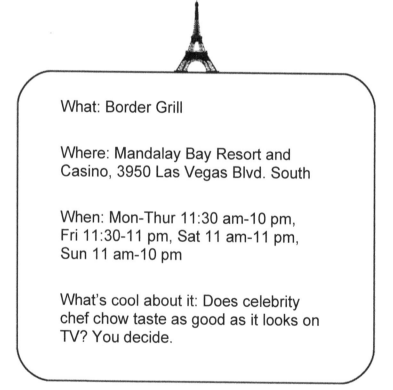

What: Border Grill

Where: Mandalay Bay Resort and Casino, 3950 Las Vegas Blvd. South

When: Mon-Thur 11:30 am-10 pm, Fri 11:30-11 pm, Sat 11 am-11 pm, Sun 11 am-10 pm

What's cool about it: Does celebrity chef chow taste as good as it looks on TV? You decide.

Joël Robuchon

The Las Vegas culinary scene has changed greatly over the last few decades. Food is no longer something cheap that you gobble down quickly between gambling sessions. The influx of star chefs from all over the world has transformed Vegas into a premier gourmet eating destination.

At the top of the heap is legendary French chef Joël Robuchon, the man the prestigious Gault Millau food guide calls the "Chef of the Century." When Robuchon came out of retirement to open his eponymous restaurant in the MGM Grand, expectations were high. He still managed to exceed them by establishing Las Vegas' first-ever Michelin 3-star restaurant in 2009.

Dinner at Joël Robuchon is not just a meal; it's a full-fledged experience. When you call to make your reservation, you will be offered a complimentary limousine ride to and from dinner. The limo will bring you to a special gated entrance to The Mansion, MGM's hotel-inside-a-hotel for high rollers and big spenders. You will have a few minutes to admire the opulent environment as you hostess brings you from the limo to the restaurant.

The dining room is richly decorated and quiet, the latter being a Vegas rarity. The intimate area can seat 60, so most of the time the incredibly accommodating staff outnumber the patrons.

Various a la carte items are available, but the full Robuchon experience can only be had from the degustation menu, a sixteen-course expression of the great chef's creativity. It begins with a bread trolley, a cart of twenty different breads, each more delicious than the last. Choose carefully, because you don't want to fill up on bread. Individual dishes arrive in a well-timed parade. You'll see caviar, lobster, veal, and many others prepared in imaginative combinations you have probably never seen before. A cart full of mignardises (dozens of unbelievably delicious small desserts) brings the extravaganza to a close.

After you have been treated like a king, you will be presented with a kingly bill. The sixteen course menu hits for $395 per person, and that's before the wine. Smaller tasting menus are available, bringing the cost down as low as $120 each. Occasional specials might bring you under the magic $100 mark.

What: Joël Robuchon

Where: MGM Grand Hotel & Casino, 3799 Las Vegas Boulevard South

When: Sun-Thur 5:30 pm-10 pm, Fri-Sat 5:30 pm-10:30 pm

What's cool about it: It hits the spot when 15 courses are just not enough.

Emeril's New Orleans Fish House

TV chef Emeril Lagasse opened his first Las Vegas restaurant in 1995 inside the MGM Grand hotel/casino. The western version of his New Orleans Fish House was an immediate success and it continues to impress. The décor is a combination of Las Vegas glitz and New Orleans hominess that makes for a welcoming dining area.

The flavor of New Orleans is here, even when they have to fly it in. The food is fresh and brought in from the Gulf coast and other parts of the country. This is especially noteworthy in the matter of seafood, as fresh seafood is notoriously difficult to find in Vegas. Whether you choose the gumbo or a seafood platter or the market fresh fish, there's something here for any fish fan.

If seafood isn't your thing, don't worry. The menu contains a nice variety of choices packed with Emeril's trademark "Bam!" The roasted quail with foie gras stuffing is a highlight, and the pecan crusted pork loin is worth a go. Make sure you leave room for dessert, since no one should be allowed to exit the restaurant without trying a slice of Emeril's banana cream pie.

There's no need to waste your time at a food court when this place is open for lunch. In addition to many of the items from the dinner menu, they offer an excellent white pizza and a nice selection of po boy sandwiches. The po boys come on toasted French bread, and feature choices like pulled pork or cornmeal fried rock shrimp.

Expect the dinner entrees to cost $30-$50, and the a la carte extras can add up. Lunch is a good bit cheaper, and that makes it a pretty solid deal.

No matter when you go, you'll find the staff to be efficient and reliably friendly. Emeril does occasionally show up at his restaurants, so there is a very small chance that you might meet the man himself.

What: Emeril's New Orleans Fish House

Where: MGM Grand Hotel & Casino, 3799 Las Vegas Boulevard South

When: 11:30 am-10 pm, daily

What's cool about it: New Orleans delights from the man with the BAM!

Firefly* Tapas Kitchen and Bar

For those unfamiliar with tapas, it is a cuisine of appetizers and small dishes that originated in Spain. Order some drinks and a couple of plates to share, and you have the beginnings of a fun evening. Add a few more plates and you can make an entire meal out of it. The selection at Firefly is not limited to Spanish dishes. Not even close. While this might upset some tapas purists, it will make your taste buds happy.

There are over 50 different choices on the menu, and there's enough variety to satisfy every member of your party. The tapas are divided into four categories.

The choices in chilled tapas include boquerones (Spanish white anchovies on toast), tuna tartare, an excellent gazpacho, or a plate of Serrano ham and Manchego cheese.

The hot tapas section is the largest section and it contains the most variety. If you're looking for something you can't find everywhere, go for the stuffed dates or the roasted eggplant cannelloni. Enjoy a mushroom tart, with boursin cheese wrapped in a puff pastry. The Manchego mac and cheese is less exotic, but it might be the most popular item on the menu.

The seafood tapas choices are headed by the delicious Firefly* fish sticks (filet of tilapia with Japanese bread crumbs). The chorizo clams and the pulpo asado (marinated and grilled octopus) are also worth a taste.

The final group contains the meat and poultry tapas. Three words. Filet mignon sliders. Try them.

Firefly features a full bar and wine by the glass. They are rightfully proud of their sangria, which is marinated for three days and served by the glass or the pitcher.

If you're looking for good food in a casual, festive atmosphere, Firefly is an excellent choice. They have locations on Paradise Rd. (not far from The Strip) and W. Sahara Ave.

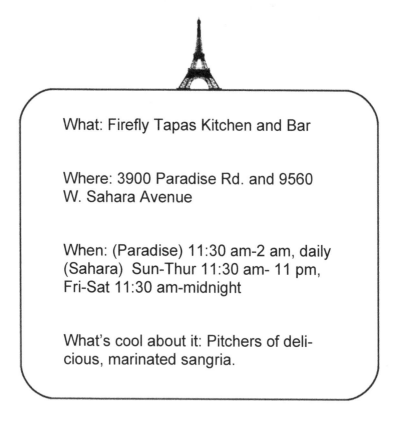

What: Firefly Tapas Kitchen and Bar

Where: 3900 Paradise Rd. and 9560 W. Sahara Avenue

When: (Paradise) 11:30 am-2 am, daily (Sahara) Sun-Thur 11:30 am- 11 pm, Fri-Sat 11:30 am-midnight

What's cool about it: Pitchers of delicious, marinated sangria.

Mon Ami Gabi

Mon Ami Gabi brings to mind the three big rules of real estate. Location. Location. Location. There are hundreds of restaurants that describe themselves as being "on The Strip." They aren't lying, but most of them are actually tucked away inside Strip hotels, a considerable distance from the hustle and bustle of Las Vegas Boulevard. Mon Ami Gabi is on The Strip. They're right there, just a few feet from the crowds that walk past Paris Las Vegas every day.

Their classic French bistro design offers you a choice of indoor or outdoor seating. While the indoor dining area is attractive and intimate, the outdoor patio is a very popular choice. The Strip-side vantage point is perfect for people watching, and offers a wonderful view of the Bellagio Fountain Show across the street. The patio is usually full, even when the temperature tops 100 degrees. Mist machines help protect patrons from the heat, and the light "breeze" from the air conditioned interior doesn't hurt.

The specialty at Mon Ami Gabi is steak. The beef is carefully selected, expertly cooked, and finished with a French flair. Whether you choose a classic béarnaise sauce, the blue cheese sauce, or the merlot butter, you're likely to be treated to one of the best steaks you have ever tasted.

Before your steak arrives, take the opportunity to enjoy some excellent soups. The French onion soup is baked with a delicious gruyére topping. The avocado and basil gazpacho might not be French, but if anyone offers you a taste of theirs, say "oui."

They offer a traditional breakfast of scratch made waffles, pancakes, crepes, and (of course) French toast. Lunchtime brings a large selection of salads, burgers and sandwiches. They also have a gluten-free menu.

At Mon Ami Gabi, dinner entrees range from $20 - $40, but you can get the same great atmosphere for a lot less if you visit for breakfast or lunch.

What: Mon Ami Gabi

Where: Paris Las Vegas, 3655 Las Vegas Boulevard South

When: Sun-Thur 7 am-11 pm, Fri-Sat 7 am-12 am

What's cool about it: Gourmet food, outdoors, in the heart of The Strip.

Carnival Court

If you're walking down The Strip and you're approaching Harrah's, that loud music and those party sounds you're hearing are probably coming from Carnival Court. The outdoor bar and concert stage are located just outside of the Harrah's casino. Carnival Court features live music daily, usually beginning in the afternoon and extending until 2 or 3 am. There is often a DJ spinning when a band isn't playing.

When the sun goes down the place really starts to jump. It functions as a type of party magnet; pulling pedestrians from the nearby sidewalk and making them part of the festivities. It's not uncommon to stop in for a drink and end up staying for half the night.

Beware of that 3-foot-tall frozen drink you just ordered. It doesn't just look funky. It might contain five or six shots of liquor. While the drinks are pricy, the bartenders have a reputation for pouring heavy shots, so you get value for your money.

Speaking of the bartenders, they're the main attraction here. Carnival Court is one of the premiere spots in the entire country to witness "flair" bartending. That's the bottle flipping, fire juggling, party starting bartending style you might remember Tom Cruise practicing in the movie "Cocktail." It's one thing to see it on a screen, but it's totally different to experience it in person. These guys are some of the best anywhere. Even when they aren't doing their flair performances, the bartenders do their best to make it a fun atmosphere.

Carnival Court is an outdoor venue, so the weather always has a chance to become an issue. While you aren't likely to have your trip foiled by rain in Las Vegas, a 110 degree day can certainly slow down a Saturday afternoon party.

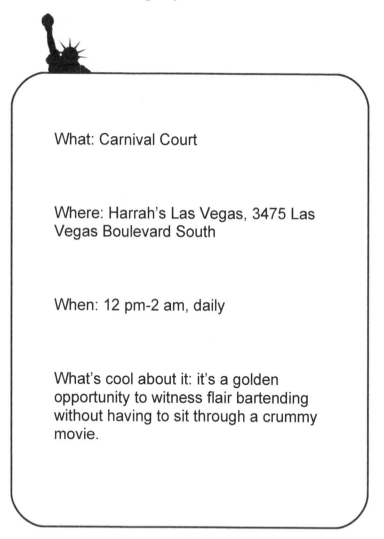

What: Carnival Court

Where: Harrah's Las Vegas, 3475 Las Vegas Boulevard South

When: 12 pm-2 am, daily

What's cool about it: it's a golden opportunity to witness flair bartending without having to sit through a crummy movie.

Hash House a Go Go

Hash House a Go Go describes its offerings as "Twisted Farm Food." What does that mean? It means heaping plates of traditional food sourced from farm fresh agriculture, made from family recipes, and served with a modern twist. It's comfort food with a gourmet flourish.

The Sage Fried Chicken & Waffles is a good representation of what you'll find here. You get two 8 oz. chicken breasts, fried with house seasoning and fresh sage. The two chicken breasts are served on top of a stack of four fresh waffles. There is a large slice of smoked Applewood bacon baked into each waffle. Yes, inside the waffle. It's livin' there. Top it off with thick maple syrup and some fried leeks, and you've got a delicious breakfast for, uh, an indeterminate number of people.

Other possibilities include a selection of house hashes, a variety of one-pound burgers, a flapjack the size of a wagon wheel, or a griddled meatloaf and mozzarella sandwich that will bring a tear to your eye.

The portions are huge, pretty much across the board. The towering Hash House creations are legendary in Vegas – and beyond. The restaurant was featured in a 2009 episode of the Travel Channel's "Man v. Food." If you're a walking stomach like Man v. Food's Adam Richman, you might be able to finish your meal. The rest of us can look forward to a rather sizable doggie bag.

They are open for breakfast, lunch and dinner, but the breakfast is what put them on the map. Many of the most popular breakfast selections are available all day long.

The location on Sahara Ave has been a big hit with locals for years, but watch out! The tourists have discovered it. To meet the demand, there are now Hash House a Go Go locations at the M Resort, Imperial Palace, and downtown at the Plaza. More are planned.

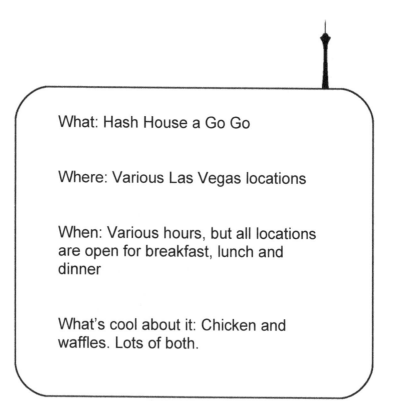

What: Hash House a Go Go

Where: Various Las Vegas locations

When: Various hours, but all locations are open for breakfast, lunch and dinner

What's cool about it: Chicken and waffles. Lots of both.

Grand Lux Café

Most major Las Vegas resorts have a 24-hour coffee shop/restaurant to serve the needs of their visitors. The Venetian is quite a bit classier than the average Vegas resort. When they were planning their 24-hour restaurant, they went to David Overton, the creator of the Cheesecake Factory, and asked him to create an upscale casual restaurant concept that matched the opulence of The Venetian. Using the finest European bistros and grand cafes as his inspiration, along with his own mega-successful restaurant chain, the result was the Grand Lux Café.

The influence of the Cheesecake Factory is apparent when you look at the enormous menu. Whether you're looking for burgers, pastas, salads, seafood, Asian food, pizzas, sandwiches, steaks or decadent desserts, the Grand Lux has what you want. We're not talking about an item or two from each category. It's more like a page or two for each type of food.

The menu features recognizable dishes with unusual twists. The double stuffed potato spring rolls are a delicious starter. The traditional crispy Asian wrapper is filled with mashed potatoes and covered in bacon and melted cheddar. From the sandwich menu, the Grand Lux Burger Melt just might be the best burger in town. Its grilled parmesan cheese bread stands up well to the melted cheddar, grilled onions and gooey dressing, but you'll probably make a mess anyway.

If you're looking for dessert, don't worry, they've got you covered. In addition to the predictable selection of Cheesecake Factory cheesecakes, there's a bakery on site, producing fresh pies, cakes and puddings all day. Another nice touch is the box of freshly-baked warm cookies (or beignets). If you order them at the beginning of your meal, they'll be hot and ready when you leave. The Grand Lux Café worked so well at the Venetian, they put a second location in the nearby Palazzo. A handful of them have begun to spring up around the country, but for most of us, Vegas is our best bet.

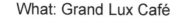

What: Grand Lux Café

Where: Venetian Hotel and Casino, 3355 Las Vegas Blvd. South; The Palazzo, 3327 Las Vegas Blvd. South

When: (Venetian) Open 24 hours, (Palazzo) Sun-Thur 6 am-2 am, Fri-Sat 6 am-3 am

What's cool about it: A massive menu, and warm cookies to go.

Delmonico Steakhouse

At first glance, the Delmonico Steakhouse doesn't look like the creation of a famous New Orleans chef. Emeril Lagasse's steak heaven looks sharp, professional, and thematically neutral. Once you open the menu, it only takes a few seconds for the Cajun and Creole influences to make themselves known.

Emeril's famous New Orleans barbecued shrimp appetizer is here, as is a delicious traditional New Orleans gumbo. Most of the items have at least a touch of Lagasse's favorite cuisine. Even the steaks have a touch of New Orleans, in the form of Emeril's signature Creole seasoning.

Speaking of steaks, the selection is much like the restaurant itself – sharp and professional. If you're looking for some transcendent new way to cut and prepare steak, you aren't going to find it here. You will find excellent cuts of prime, aged beef, which are cooked to perfection. Of special note is the bone-in ribeye, for those who love their steaks extra large and delicious.

The service is responsive and over-the-top friendly. If you want to put your team to work, they will toss an excellent Caesar salad at your tableside. If you choose the chateaubriand, you can watch them carve it at your table.

They are open for lunch and dinner. The lunch menu features a simpler selection, highlighted by delectable pot roast that is so tender you can cut it with a fork. Lunch is also a great time to grab a slice of Emeril's famous banana cream pie.

The Delmonico Steakhouse is located in the Venetian Hotel and Casino. Lunch entrees range from $14-$19. Dinner is a good bit steeper, with an entree spread of $36-$55. Salads and sides are extra.

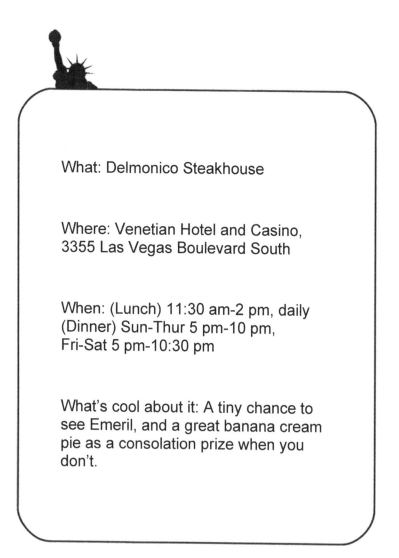

What: Delmonico Steakhouse

Where: Venetian Hotel and Casino, 3355 Las Vegas Boulevard South

When: (Lunch) 11:30 am-2 pm, daily (Dinner) Sun-Thur 5 pm-10 pm, Fri-Sat 5 pm-10:30 pm

What's cool about it: A tiny chance to see Emeril, and a great banana cream pie as a consolation prize when you don't.

Lavo

What is Lavo? The answer varies, depending on what time of day or night you go there. At dinner time it's a dinner place, serving up some of the town's best Italian fare. Starting at 10 PM, and extending well into the early hours, it is one of Las Vegas' most popular night clubs.

First, the restaurant. There is a tendency for Las Vegas restaurants to complicate seemingly simple things. Italian food is one of them. There is no great need to invent a new way to serve Italian food every few months. Lavo understands this. They do Italian food in a straightforward manner, and the results are delicious.

They'll start you with some complimentary garlic bread that has all the garlic and butter you could possibly want. If you take a chance on the Kobe meatball, expect it to be enormous and fantastic. Don't expect to finish it yourself. The same thing goes for the tasty, thin crust pizzas that are two feet long!

If you leave room for dessert, you've probably done something wrong, but in this case, you will be richly rewarded for your misdeed. A tremendous chocolate bread pudding or a serving of deep fried Oreos awaits you, along with a nice selection of coffees.

The Lavo night club is upscale and intimate – which means "kind of small," especially if you're talking about the dance floor. The Mediterranean bath house décor gives it a unique atmosphere.

Expect lines on the weekend. The rich and famous come here, so if you want to get through the front door, you have to make an effort. Shorts and t-shirts aren't going to cut it.

Lavo clings to the not-very-secret rule of successful clubs. There is no party if there are no women. Ladies get treated well here. Reduced or free admission is the norm, and an open bar for women is common.

What: Lavo

Where: The Palazzo, 3327 Las Vegas Boulevard South

When: (Restaurant) Sun-Thur 5 pm-12 am (Nightclub) Sun, Tue, Wed, Fri, Sat 10:30 pm-5 am

What's cool about it: Kobe meatballs as big as softballs.

Bellagio Fountain Show

The best free show in town can be seen every afternoon and evening in front of the Bellagio Hotel and Casino. At least twice every hour the beautiful nine-acre lake in front of the Bellagio comes alive with a wonderful display of light, music and water.

The fountains are an engineering marvel. The show requires over 4500 lights and 1200 water jets. Many of the jets are subtle – they move and sway with a full range of spherical motion that makes the water appear to dance. Others are known as "shooters," with some capable of blasting a column of water 460 feet into the air.

The moving water is choreographed to a wide variety of musical choices, from Gene Kelly and Frank Sinatra to Faith Hill and Celine Dion. During the Christmas season, a handful of holiday tunes are added to the mix. There's no telling which song you'll get next. You just have to show up and see.

The combination of artistry and technology works perfectly. The result is something that should not be missed. Plan to stay for multiple shows, since each one is different.

The Bellagio is located pretty much in the center of The Strip. The lake is right in front of it. You can't miss it. The show runs from 3 p.m. until midnight on Monday through Friday, and noon until midnight on the weekend. There's a new show every 30 minutes in the afternoon, and every 15 minutes from 8 p.m. to midnight. Poor weather, most notably wind, can cancel some shows, but it happens quite rarely.

The show is best seen from the railing surrounding the lake. You might have to wait for one show to end to get a place at the railing, but it's worth it.

What: Bellagio Fountain Show

Where: In the giant lake in front of the Bellagio, 3600 Las Vegas Blvd. South

When: Mon-Fri 3 pm-12 am, Sat-Sun 12 pm-12 am

What's cool about it: Fountains blasting over 400 feet into the air, but in an artful, relaxing way.

Bellagio Lobby and Conservatory

After taking in one or two of the excellent Bellagio Fountain shows, take the opportunity to step inside the property. There's more cool stuff to see, and it's absolutely free.

As you enter the Bellagio lobby, your eye will inevitably be drawn to a work called Fiori di Como, a sprawling, multi-colored glass sculpture that fills much of the lobby's ceiling. The sculpture is the work of artist Dale Chihuly, and it is comprised of over 2000 hand-blown glass flowers. It covers over 2000 square feet of ceiling and contains over 40,000 pounds of glass, making it the largest glass sculpture in the world. A gift shop featuring more of Chihuly's wonderful work is located nearby.

Continue through the lobby and you will emerge in the Bellagio's majestic conservatory and botanical gardens. Beautiful plants and trees are bathed in natural light. Thousands of flowers paint the room with color. Choreographed bursts of dancing water arc through the air. Artfully arranged gazebos, bridges, and ponds serve to complete the current theme.

The arrangement changes five times a year; once for each season, and again for the Chinese New Year. It's a bit more complicated than dragging the Christmas decorations out of the attic, though. A team of 140 caretakers are charged with creating and maintaining each display, and hand-watering most of the plants. The 10,000 potted flowers are switched out every two weeks to maintain the bright and fresh feel.

The Conservatory is open 24/7, every day of the year, except for a few days of downtime when they are transitioning to the next theme. It is one of the most popular spots in town, and an especially popular photography subject. The sheer bulk of photographers can make it difficult to walk from one end of the garden to the other. Be careful or you'll end up with a walk-on role in a stranger's vacation snapshots.

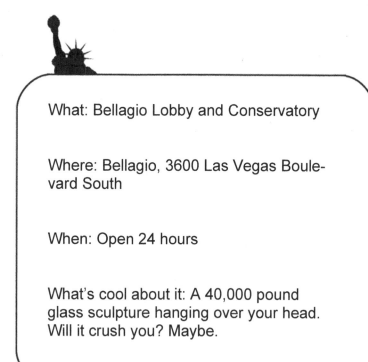

What: Bellagio Lobby and Conservatory

Where: Bellagio, 3600 Las Vegas Boulevard South

When: Open 24 hours

What's cool about it: A 40,000 pound glass sculpture hanging over your head. Will it crush you? Maybe.

The Show in the Sky

For years, the Masquerade in the Sky show was a mainstay at the Rio Hotel and Casino. The free show at the Rio has been revamped and relaunched as The Show in the Sky, with a more contemporary feel. A lot of the details remain from the old Masquerade show. It still takes place in the Masquerade Village, which is smack dab in the middle of the casino, though you can watch it from the second floor shopping area. There are still about a dozen singers and dancers (half men, half women). They still perform on a large two-tiered stage, complete with spiral staircases on each end.

The old Mardi Gras theme is gone, and in its place is a show with a more adult feel. Much of the female costuming is provided by Victoria's Secret, and one of the productions uses a 17-foot-long bed.

The musical numbers are upbeat and fun. The enthusiasm of the dancers goes a long way in making up for not-quite-perfect coordination.

With only a stage show, you might be wondering why they call it The Show in the Sky. Things become clearer when you look up. As the show progresses, a series of colorfully lit floats parade above the crowd. More costumed entertainers are on the floats. Some might even toss you a beaded necklace (a nice nod to the old Mardi Gras theme).

If you look up at the floats and think, "I wanna ride in one of those," you can do that. Tickets are $12.95, and should be purchased at least 30 minutes before the show starts. Spaces are limited, because putting 50 people in a float has Hindenburg written all over it.

The Show in the Sky is free. It runs Thursday through Saturday, every hour on the hour from 6 PM to 11 PM. There are three different productions, so if you stay a while you can see three shows in one night.

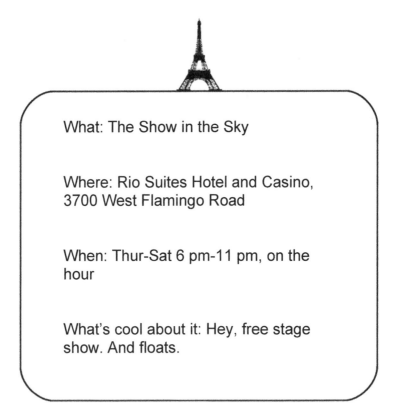

What: The Show in the Sky

Where: Rio Suites Hotel and Casino, 3700 West Flamingo Road

When: Thur-Sat 6 pm-11 pm, on the hour

What's cool about it: Hey, free stage show. And floats.

Mirage Aquarium and Atrium

The Mirage Hotel and Casino has two free attractions that are available just as you walk through the front door.

As you step indoors from the harsh sun of the desert, you'll be surrounded by a lush, tropical rain forest. Palm trees soar over sixty feet above your head. Waterfalls cascade into a lovely manmade lagoon. A huge variety of flowers, including over 300 orchids and 1000 bromeliads, line your path. You can even feel a light mist in the air, and that can be a pretty welcome feeling after a day in the outdoor heat.

All of this happens beneath a 100-foot dome designed to let in plenty of natural light. There are 100 different types of plant in all, and it requires four full-time gardeners to help them thrive and survive. The gentle mist is provided by a computerized watering system. If you're not a fan of humidity, don't worry. It's not a muggy kind of mist. It succeeds in keeping both you and the plants cool.

The other cool attraction can be found directly behind the hotel front desk – a 20,000 gallon saltwater aquarium. The tank is 53 feet long, 8 feet tall, and 6 feet from front to back. Inside you will find almost 1000 creatures, each specially chosen to live in harmony with their environment and each other. Sharks and stingrays swim peacefully with eels and puffer fish. All of it happens against the backdrop of vibrant, colorful coral that was designed to bring to mind Australia's Great Barrier Reef.

Even if you aren't checking into the hotel you'll want to take some time to admire the aquatic work of art. Don't worry. The people working the check-in desk will understand.

What: Mirage Aquarium and Atrium

Where: The Mirage, 3400 Las Vegas Boulevard South

When: Open 24 hours

What's cool about it: Beautiful plants, cool mist, and a big, glass wall full of fish.

The Volcano

In 1989, The Mirage introduced an attraction the likes of which Las Vegas had never seen before – a volcano that erupted hourly, filling the night with light, sound and fire. Over the years, millions of visitors have flocked to witness the recurring disaster (The volcano. Not the various Britney Spears comeback concerts.). The volcano has become one of the iconic sights of Las Vegas.

If you've never seen the volcano, or haven't seen it in a while, now is the time to do it. The Mirage completed a big time upgrade in 2008. The upgraded volcano was masterminded by WET, the brains behind the Bellagio Fountain Show. It features choreographed fire shooters that send massive fireballs into the air, and a new state of the art sound system. Grateful Dead drummer and Rock and Roll Hall of Fame member Mickey Hart and Indian tabla musician Zakir Hussain were called in to upgrade the musical soundtrack that accompanies each eruption. As you might imagine, the all-new volcano is heavy on percussion, and the result is awesome. The volcano rocks!

Eruptions happen every hour on the hour, nightly after dark, as long as the weather cooperates (in Las Vegas that usually means the wind). The show is free, just in front of The Mirage at the northern/central part of The Strip. No tickets are required. You can walk up and watch it. Get there 5 – 10 minutes before the hour, so you can get a good, close viewing position. If you do it right, you should be able to feel the heat from the fire!

If you're staying in The Mirage, or across the street at The Venetian, The Palazzo, or Harrah's, you can get a great look at the show from a strip-facing room on an upper floor.

What: The Volcano

Where: The Mirage, 3400 Las Vegas Boulevard South

When: 6 pm-11 pm, every night, on the hour

What's cool about it: Blows up good. Blows up *real* good.

The Sirens of TI

In 1959, director Ed Wood created a film called "Plan 9 from Outer Space". It wasn't simply a bad movie. Over time, it grew to be considered the worst movie ever made. It is screened regularly for people who gather to mock its badness. They take great joy in laughing at its ineptitude.

Treasure Island brought us the Las Vegas version of "Plan 9" in 2003, when they replaced the enormously popular Buccaneer Bay Pirate Battle with a new production – The Sirens of TI. It has all of the same mechanics of its predecessor - two ships, pirates, stunts, flames and explosions, but that's where the similarities end.

Instead of fighting the British, the pirates are confronted with a shipload of beautiful women dressed in lingerie (the titular Sirens). The pirates might think they have encountered easy prey, but their ship is eventually sunk, presumably by horrible acting and excruciating dialogue. Although the cheesy lip-synched musical numbers could also have had a hand in it.

Appreciating the show requires the correct mindset. If you went into a showing of "Plan 9" thinking that you were getting "Citizen Kane", you wouldn't be happy when you left the theater. The same concept applies here. If you're expecting something good, you'll be disappointed. If you're expecting something cringeworthy, you'll be entertained by its awfulness.

The show is free, right in front of the Treasure Island Hotel and Casino (at the northern end of center Strip). Shows are nightly at 7, 8:30 and 10. There's a

5:30 show in the winter and an 11:30 show in the summer. Get there about 15-20 minutes early for the best view, and be prepared for a possible cancellation if it's very windy. There are scads of scantily-clad women and lame attempts at sexual innuendo, so you have to decide if your kids can take it. They'll probably like the explosions, though.

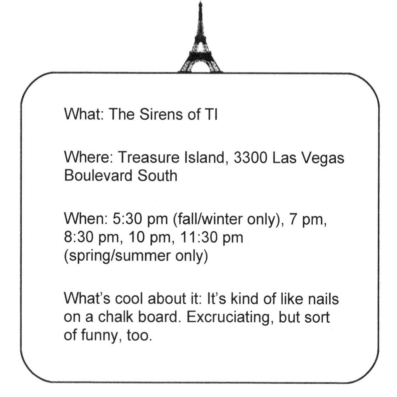

What: The Sirens of TI

Where: Treasure Island, 3300 Las Vegas Boulevard South

When: 5:30 pm (fall/winter only), 7 pm, 8:30 pm, 10 pm, 11:30 pm (spring/summer only)

What's cool about it: It's kind of like nails on a chalk board. Excruciating, but sort of funny, too.

The Best View in Town

Some large cities might have a problem with traffic or crime, but when you come to Las Vegas your greatest danger might come from your fellow visitors. Imagine this: You're in a crowd (which in Las Vegas is pretty much all the time). You're walking past something cool. Suddenly, the person walking in front of you comes to a dead stop. No warning. No heads up. He just stops. If you don't take some sort of evasive action, you're going to smash right into him.

Human fender benders and near misses happen all the time in Las Vegas. Why? The city is a feast for the eyes. There is such a wealth of sites and attractions, people are always stopping to gawk, to snap a picture, or just because they can't believe their eyes.

One of the best places to stop is on the south end of The Strip. It's a walking bridge that crosses over Las Vegas Boulevard, linking the New York New York to the MGM Grand. The view is amazing at any time, but it is best at night.

On one side of the street is the MGM Grand, an enormous 5000-room behemoth that glows Emerald City green. A giant bronze lion guards the entrance. It is 45 feet tall and weighs a mere 50 tons.

Across the street is the New York New York skyline, complete with an Empire State Building, a Brooklyn Bridge, and a 1/3 scale replica of the Statue of Liberty. A roller coaster zips between the monuments.

Look south and you'll see the Luxor, an enormous 30-story-tall black pyramid. The top of the Luxor sports one of the brightest lights ever created, sending a 42 billion candle power beam straight into the sky. On a clear night, it can be seen from 250 miles away, but you're a lot closer.

Finally, to the north, is the rest of the Las Vegas Strip, with Vegas's versions of Paris, Rome and Hollywood lit up brighter than the originals.

It's a lot to see, so stop and take it all in. But first make sure that someone isn't walking right behind you.

What: The Best View in Town

Where: The bridge between New York New York and MGM Grand, 3790 Las Vegas Boulevard South

When: Open 24 hours

What's cool about it: The best place to appreciate the bright lights and the pure excess of The Strip.

Binion's Million Dollar Photo Op

For close to five decades, the Binion's casino in downtown Las Vegas was the home to one of the most popular attractions in town. Visitors could have their photograph taken while posing with an impressive display of one million dollars in cash.

The original display featured one-hundred $10,000 bills. The U.S. Treasury Department stopped distributing $10,000 bills in 1969, and the bills became rarer with each passing year. As a result, the Binion's million grew to be worth many times the face value of the bills.

That might sound pretty nice for Binion's, but it turned out to be a bit of a curse. It actually costs money to display money. As the replacement value of the rare bills soared, so did the cost of insuring the very public display. A financially strapped Binion's sold the bills to a collector in 2000.

It took them a few years, but they have finally revived the popular photo op. The new attraction takes a different route to a million dollars. Instead of the simple elegance of 100 bills, this display contains $270,000 in $100 bills, $688,000 in twenties, and $42,000 in ones. It's a big pile of money. They stack it tall, inside a five-tiered acrylic pyramid, on top of a green felt poker table. The bills might not be as rare, but the presentation makes quite a picture.

If you want to pose with the big stack of cash, you'll find Binion's on Fremont Street downtown. They'll take your picture for free. Since it's cool and it's free and it's Vegas, there's likely to be a line. Plan to wait a few minutes, especially during the busy evening hours. It's a small price to pay for a picture that will be on your Facebook page forever.

What: Binion's Million Dollar Photo Op

Where: Binion's Gambling Hall & Hotel, 128 E. Fremont Street

When: 10 am-11 pm, daily

What's cool about it: A million dollars. Did you read the part about a million dollars?

Wildlife Habitat at the Flamingo

What happens in Vegas... can be exhausting. The city's nonstop menu of excitement and fun can leave visitors searching for a place to take a moment to rest and recharge their vacation batteries.

The Flamingo hotel and casino is right in the middle of all of the noise and craziness of The Strip. So you wouldn't guess that their "backyard" was one of the quietest, most relaxing places in town.

The 15 acre Wildlife Habitat at the Flamingo is a serene garden of waterfalls, lagoons, and tropical plants from around the world. As you walk in the shade of the magnolias and palms, it's easy to forget the epic traffic jam just a few hundred yards away. Paths wind lazily through the foliage, and there are plenty of benches for weary travelers.

Swans and ducks coast over the water, while koi and goldfish swim underneath. Turtles sun themselves on rocks, and over 300 exotic birds are free to wander. If you're any good at that sort of thing, you might identify pheasants, cranes, parrots, quails and ibis among the inhabitants. You can identify an ibis at twenty paces. Can't you? Even if you're lousy at bird identification, you won't be able to miss the trademark flock of Chilean pink flamingos.

Flamingos at the Flamingo? That's got vacation photo op written all over it.

The Wildlife Habitat is open 7 days a week during daylight hours. There is no admission. Just walk right up and stay as long as you like. You don't have to be a guest at the Flamingo to enjoy their tropical paradise. However, if you are a guest at the Flamingo, you can also splash around in their nearby pool area, which is one of the most excellent in town.

What: Wildlife Habitat at the Flamingo

Where: Flamingo Las Vegas, 3555 Las Vegas Boulevard South

When: 8 am – dusk, daily

What's cool about it: Exotic birds in a peaceful landscape.

Paris Las Vegas Sights

After the success of New York New York on the south end of The Strip, it was only a matter of time before another "city" was established in Las Vegas. Paris Las Vegas joined the ranks of amazing Las Vegas sights in 1999. Paris, France is known as the City of Lights. Paris Las Vegas holds its own in the light department with its huge neon logo sign in the shape of a hot air balloon, and a half-scale replica of the Eiffel Tower that lights up the Vegas sky.

In addition to the omnipresent Eiffel Tower, the front entrance features a two-thirds-scale version of the Arc de Triomphe and a majestic and highly photographable version of La Fontaine des Mers.

The property is filled with French ambience. Excellent architectural bits include replica facades of some of the most notable Parisian buildings. In various places you will find detailed replicas of The Louvre, The Hotel de Ville, and The Paris Opera House. Once inside, you can take a walk across the Vegas version of the world famous Alexander III Bridge. As you look down from the bridge, you can see the casino area. Three legs of the Eiffel Tower actually extend right into the casino. Very cool.

Le Boulevard is the Paris shopping area. Its cobblestone streets are lit by actual brass streetlamps. The people who run the wonderful selection of small shops here are not rude, but if you're looking for full authenticity, you might be able to get them to fake it.

There's a lot to see at Paris, but there's also a lot to see from Paris. The Eiffel Tower is fifty stories tall, and provides an incredible view of the center Strip. Watching the Bellagio Fountain Show across the street is always great, but watching it from 460 feet in the air is like nothing else. Tickets to the top of the Tower are $10.50 during the day or $15.50 at night, and include a scenic elevator ride to the top.

What: Paris Las Vegas Sights

Where: Paris Las Vegas, 3655 Las Vegas Boulevard South

When: Open 24 hours

What's cool about it: If you stare at the resort in a menacing way, they just might surrender it to you.

The Lion Habitat at MGM Grand

The lion has been the symbol of MGM for decades, going all the way back to Leo, whose roar has kicked off countless MGM films. The MGM Grand salutes the lion with their Lion Habitat, a free exhibit at the MGM Grand property.

On the other side of the 1.5 inch thick soundproof glass is a 5345 square foot habitat of rocks, greenery and waterfalls. Oh, and lions. There is also a viewing tunnel that passes through the habitat. Some parts of the tunnel have a glass ceiling, which also serves as a platform for the lions. If you're lucky enough to have one pass above you, you'll get a unique view of the lion, and a close-up idea of just how gigantic their paws are.

There are over three dozen MGM lions in total, permanently residing at an 8.5 acre ranch 12 miles out of town. A few animals are brought into the habitat daily, where they are displayed for just a part of the day, before being returned to the ranch.

How cool is this exhibit? That depends on a lot of things. The quantity and type of lions varies greatly. You might get one big, majestic male lion that isn't in the mood to do much but sleep. You might get a handful of younger lions that are jumping around and playing constantly. It's luck of the draw. You might get a chance to see them feeding, or playing with their trainers. You will most likely get a chance to get very close to a lion, which is always cool.

Your fellow tourists are also a factor. The crowd around the exhibit can become large, so it might take some time and effort to get yourself a good viewing spot.

Be warned! While the exhibit is free, your trip to see the lions might not be. The nearby gift shop sells a nice variety of lion wear and furry lion toys. You might also be faced with the opportunity to have your photo taken while feeding a lion cub. If you or someone in your group craves the photo op, the price is $25.

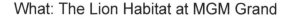

What: The Lion Habitat at MGM Grand

Where: MGM Grand Hotel & Casino, 3799 Las Vegas Boulevard South

When: 11 am-7 pm, daily, feedings at 11:15 am and 4:30 pm

What's cool about it: Getting two inches away from a bunch of lions.

Welcome to Las Vegas Sign

No trip to Las Vegas would be complete without a visit to the Las Vegas sign. You've seen it in movies and on TV, but if you're wondering if it really exists, the answer is yes. The iconic sign, which reads "Welcome to Fabulous Las Vegas Nevada" on the front and "Drive Carefully Come Back Soon" on the back, is one of the prime photo opportunities in a town filled with them.

For most of the years since the sign's erection in 1959, visitors had to make a slightly death-defying dash across 50 mph Las Vegas Boulevard traffic to reach the safety of the median. That changed in 2008, when a shiny new parking area was installed near the sign. The mini lot has a dozen spaces for cars and two for buses.

The ambiance is not the greatest. Between the cars zipping past on both sides, and the sounds of jet engines from the very nearby airport, it can be a bit noisy. But what do you expect? It was designed as a road sign, not a tourist destination.

There is often a small crowd of people around the sign, but they're all there to do the same thing you are. They snap their pictures and move on, which makes the unofficial "line" move pretty quickly. You can frequently find an Elvis impersonator or a similar costumed oddity willing to pose with you. They work for tips, so treat them kindly.

What's the best time to go? It's your call, really. The sign lights up at night, but you get a perfectly good view during the day. The sign shows up better at night.

The people standing in front of it show up better in daylight.

You'll find the sign in the median at 5100 Las Vegas Boulevard South. That's the south end of The Strip, a few blocks past Mandalay Bay. You can walk it if you like, but it's a pretty cheap cab ride from the South Strip properties, and most cabbies will wait while you snap your pictures.

What: Welcome to Las Vegas Sign

Where: On The Strip, about half a mile south of Mandalay Bay

When: Open 24 hours

What's cool about it: Possibly the most famous sign in the world.

The Forum Shops

Referring to the Forum Shops at Caesars Palace as a mall doesn't do it justice. Yes, technically it's a collection of retail stores where people can shop, just like in your city. But that's where the resemblance ends. This is a different kind of mall.

The décor and architecture are spectacular. High, arched ceilings give it a feeling of enormity. Marble statues, fountains and Roman columns remind you that you're in Caesars Palace. Cloud-painted blue skies lighten and darken as the day progresses. A spiral escalator carries you from one gorgeous level to another. Among these stunning surroundings, there is shopping.

Many of the shops are upscale. Big time upscale. The kinds of places that can be described with one name. Armani. Burberry. Fendi. Gucci. Bvlgari. We're talking about that kind of place, and not just a few of them, either. If you're looking for a pair of shoes, and your shoe budget resembles the average person's car budget, you still have to decide between Jimmy Choo, Louis Vuitton or Stuart Weitzman.

That's not to say the entire place is for zillion-aires. For most of us, shops like Cartier and Tiffany & Co. are great for gawking, but Banana Republic and The Gap are more our speed. That's fine. With over 160 stores, there are shops for virtually every taste and price range. The massive, three-story H&M store is the largest in the world.

Even if you don't spend a penny eating or shopping, there's plenty to do here. Just admiring the sites can take a couple of hours. The Festival of Fountains show, a.k.a. the Moving Statues show, has been a Forum Shops mainstay since 1992. The statues of the Roman gods begin to move and speak, every hour on the hour.

At the other end of the Shops, in front of the Cheesecake Factory, is another show that features moving statues – The Fall of Atlantis. The statues are a good bit more advanced in this show, and there are impressive fire and water effects to boot. This show also runs at the top of each hour.

Check out the 50,000 gallon saltwater aquarium next to The Fall of Atlantis. It features a nice variety of tropical fish and small sharks. Twice daily (1:15 p.m. and 5:15 p.m.) you can see a diver enter the tank to feed the fish. Both shows and the aquarium are part of the mall. There is no admission charge to view them.

What: The Forum Shops

Where: Caesars Palace, 3570 Las Vegas Boulevard South

When: Sun-Thur 10 am-11 pm, Fri-Sat 10 am-midnight

What's cool about it: Moving statues and crazy shopping.

The Grand Canal Shoppes

The Venetian is one of the grandest resorts on the planet. The massive, 4000-suite hotel casino was built with the influence of old Venice in mind. Nowhere is that influence more obvious than in the Grand Canal Shoppes.

A replica of St. Mark's Square is the centerpiece of the Shoppes, complete with a painted sky that soars 70 feet above the action. Visitors can stroll amongst "buildings" designed to resemble those in Venice, and an actual navigable canal runs parallel to the shops. Singing gondoliers escort their passengers along the waterway, and you can join them for a ride. Street performers and opera singers ply their respective crafts. Elaborately made-up actors portray marble statues so convincingly you might not notice they're alive.

Within this charming environment is a shopping mall of remarkable diversity. The fine photography of the Peter Lik Gallery and high-end watches of Movado exist side by side with more traditional mall favorites like Ann Taylor and Brookstone. Specialty shops offer everything from blown glass figurines to Faberge eggs. The restaurant selection is large and equally eclectic. If celebrity chefs are your thing, try Wolfgang Puck's Postrio or Mario Batali's OTTO pizzeria. If you're looking for a good old fashioned food court, the Canal Shoppes have a nice, big one, with Johnny Rockets, Nathan's hot dogs, Panda Express and Haagen Dazs among the choices.

The Shoppes are a quarter mile from end to end, so whether you're walking or in a gondola it'll take you some time to see it all. If this just isn't enough shopping for you, the Shoppes at The Palazzo are right next door, with upscale shopping at Barneys New York, Manolo Blahnik, Ralph Lauren and Michael Kors, to name a few.

What: The Grand Canal Shoppes

Where: Venetian Hotel and Casino, 3355 Las Vegas Boulevard South

When: Sun-Thur 10 am-11 pm, Fri-Sat 10 am-midnight

What's cool about it: Try out your stand-up comedy, and see if you can make one of the human statues smile.

Fashion Show Mall

If shopping is a big part of your vacation experience, then you won't want to miss a trip to the Fashion Show Mall. It's a huge indoor shopping mall at the north end of The Strip. When you see the giant gray disc that looks like a flying saucer, you're seeing the entrance of the Fashion Show Mall.

Many visitors to Fashion Show note that it doesn't seem as crowded as most other malls, but that isn't due to a lack of shoppers. There are thousands of people inside the mall at any given time, but they are dwarfed by the immense scale of the place. The 250+ stores and 7 anchors (Bloomingdale's Home, Dillard's, Forever 21, Macy's, Neiman Marcus, Nordstrom, and Saks Fifth Avenue) are spread across nearly 2 million square feet of space. Just walking around here counts as your exercise for the day.

It's basically the mall in your home town on steroids. It's all the stores you have, plus all the stores you wish you had. Looking for shoes? There are over 40 places that sell them, so you can afford to be choosy. How about a bite to eat? You have over three dozen choices in the mammoth food court.

Why do they call it the Fashion Show Mall? Show up at the right time and you'll see. An 80-foot retractable runway will emerge from the floor, the lights will dim, and a professional fashion show will ensue. The shows are hosted by merchants in the mall, so if you see something you like, you can go and buy it immediately. With the enormous variety of fashions available in the mall, the various stores combine to stage over 1000 runway shows per year. The fashion shows are held on Friday, Saturday and Sunday, every hour on the hour, from noon until 6 PM.

What: Fashion Show Mall

Where: 3200 Las Vegas Blvd. South

When: Mon-Sat 10 am-9 pm,
Sun 11 am-7 pm

What's cool about it: The fashion shows are a unique twist, but the sheer hugeness of the place is amazing.

Bonanza Gifts

Virtually every hotel and casino in town provides a gift shop. Walk around Las Vegas for any time at all and you'll find a passel of places to purchase a souvenir. You can choose to shop in any of these places, but why settle for second best? And since you're in Las Vegas, why settle for small? Bonanza Gifts has been a landmark at the north end of the Strip since 1980. It bills itself as the world's largest gift shop, and they're serious about it. When you walk into the store you're faced with 40,000 square feet of merchandise. That's about half the size of your average Walmart.

Not surprisingly, Bonanza is the home of all things Vegas. They have a selection of Las Vegas t-shirts that seems to go on for miles. There are Las Vegas books, Las Vegas snow globes, Las Vegas pillows, and a comprehensive selection of fuzzy dice for your rearview mirror. If you're looking for gambling supplies, they can set you up with dice, poker chips, or an electric card shuffler.

They have playing cards that were used in actual casinos. The cards are notched, just in case you get the bright idea of sneaking a couple of aces into the poker room, but they're the real thing. Decks from most of the Strip hotels are represented.

They also have a wide selection of gag gifts. Sure, you can buy yourself a whoopee cushion or a rubber chicken, but for pure obnoxiousness, it's tough to beat Polly the Insulting Parrot. Polly is motion sensitive, and if you walk past him he will speak to you. Polly's vocabulary is pretty rough. He might not be the vilest toy on Earth, but he's a solid contender. If Polly is up and squawking, steer the kids to another part of the store.

Bonanza Gifts has the combination of cheesiness and excess you would expect in a Las Vegas gift shop. They're open from 8 a.m. to midnight, 363 days a year.

What: Bonanza Gifts

Where: 2440 Las Vegas Boulevard South

When: 8 am-midnight, daily

What's cool about it: We dare you not to laugh at the stupid, foul-mouthed parrot.

The Fremont Street Experience

The Las Vegas tourist spots can pretty much be divided into Old Vegas (downtown) and New Vegas (The Strip). As The Strip grew and gained prominence, the older downtown locations saw their existence threatened. Ten downtown hotel/casinos got together and came up with the Fremont Street Experience (FSE). When most cities launch a type of "revitalize downtown" project the results usually range between failure and spectacular, incredibly expensive failure. The Fremont Street Experience actually works.

It works because it's fun. Think New Orleans. FSE doesn't have a Mardi Gras theme, or any theme at all, but it has the rambling, casual, anyone-is-welcome feel of a good party. There is drinking. There is noise. There is music. In the summer there are bikini-clad women who will sell you gigantic frozen drinks. And of course, there is the canopy.

When you mention FSE, most people think of the canopy – a four block long half-pipe that hangs 90 feet above the pedestrian mall portion of Fremont Street. During the day it does little more than protect you from the sun, but at night the canopy comes to life. More than 2 million LED lights turn it into a gigantic video screen over 1 ½ football fields long.

Here's how it happens. After dusk, at the top of each hour, the lights on the casino facades go dark. Then the canopy lights come on, and 550,000 watts of stereo sound comes with them. Each show features a song, or a medley of songs. Popular selections include "American

Pie" by Don McLean, and individual shows featuring the music of KISS, Queen and The Doors. Each musical piece is accompanied by an impressive collection of animated graphics created to complement the music. Ten minutes later, the show ends and the party resumes. FSE also features live bands most nights. Kiosks and small shops sell souvenirs and other items of interest. Performance artists and people in costume wander freely. If you're looking for champagne and caviar, this isn't it. If you're looking for a fun night out, it's definitely worth a try.

They also added an 800 foot zipline in 2010. For $15-20 you can fly above the crowd at speeds of up to 25 mph. The zipline is a temporary setup, but there is a plan to increase its length and make it permanent.

There is no admission charge for FSE. Just walk right up and you're a part of it.

What: Fremont Street Experience

Where: Fremont Street, downtown

When: Open 24 hours, hourly light shows at night

What's cool about it: It's a nonstop party, with a light show every hour.

Madame Tussauds

If you want to see famous people in Las Vegas, you can take your chances haunting the trendy clubs or you can go for the sure thing. You can see Brad Pitt, Britney Spears, Johnny Depp, Lady Gaga, Oprah Winfrey and dozens more at Madame Tussauds in The Venetian.

Madame Tussauds is the world famous wax museum based in London, but with an extensive collection of incredibly lifelike sculptures on display in Las Vegas. Just getting a chance to see the wax creations is fun enough, but many of the displays are interactive.

The Tiger Woods display shows Tiger studying a putt, but you get to grab a club, step up and sink it. As your putt rolls into the hole the crowd goes wild!

Only the hottest of the hot get to hang with Hugh Hefner. But now you can grab a drink, put on some Playboy bunny ears, and hop into bed with a pajamaed Hef.

You can also sing karaoke for Simon Cowell, step into the octagon with mixed martial arts legend Chuck Liddell, or play PVC percussion instruments with the guys from Blue Man Group.

One of the most popular attractions is the "Marry Clooney" display. Women (or men, if they like) get to put on a wedding dress and pose for pictures with a tuxedoed George Clooney as the groom.

If you have your eye on getting married to someone besides George, that's OK too. The Clooney display also serves as a real wedding chapel. The wedding ceremony package comes with two wax "witnesses." Want to get married with Evel Knievel and Snoop Dogg acting as witnesses? Madame Tussauds can make it happen.

Admission is $25 for adults, $18 for seniors, or $15 for children 7-12. You can knock 20% off the ticket price by purchasing online. Bring your camera.

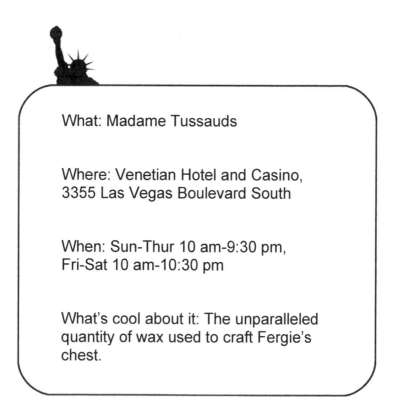

What: Madame Tussauds

Where: Venetian Hotel and Casino, 3355 Las Vegas Boulevard South

When: Sun-Thur 10 am-9:30 pm, Fri-Sat 10 am-10:30 pm

What's cool about it: The unparalleled quantity of wax used to craft Fergie's chest.

The Auto Collections

The Auto Collections at Imperial Palace is a lot of things at once. It's kind of a museum and kind of a sales floor. Some of the cars are amazingly old and others are much more recent. Some are priceless and others are quite affordable. Even the price of admission can vary.

Here's how it works. On the fifth floor of the Imperial Palace are 125,000 square feet of cool cars. Really cool cars. Even seasoned car buffs will find cars they've never seen before. There are about 250-300 different cars at any given time. The collection resembles a museum in that you have an unlimited amount of time to walk from car to car, and there is a friendly staff of car nuts who will gladly tell you everything they know about the machines.

Unlike a museum, most of the cars here are for sale. Some, like the 1939 Chrysler Royal Sedan in which Johnny Carson learned to drive, are for display only, but most of them are just waiting to become part of your collection.

You might find a 1934 Rolls Royce Phantom II or a 1954 Alfa Rome 1900 SS Ghia or a 1961 Chevrolet Corvette 283/245 Roadster. Or you might find none of the above. Since the cars are on sale, the composition of the collection turns over constantly. It's a different collection every time you visit, and they're constantly looking to acquire interesting road machines.

The showroom is open 7 days a week. Admission is $8.95 for adults or $5.00 for senior and children. That is, if you choose to pay it. Staying at the Imperial

Palace will get you free admission. So will an AAA membership. A military ID will do it too. There are also free entry coupons at autocollections.com. You can print out and use as many as you like. With only a little planning you can see one of the greatest car collections on Earth for free.

As you enter, they urge you to take all the pictures you like. The lighting is excellent, so you should take them up on the offer.

What: The Auto Collections

Where: Imperial Palace, 3535 Las Vegas Boulevard South

When: 10 am-6 pm, daily

What's cool about it: A dozen Rolls Royces are great, but where else can you find them displayed next to a Yugo?

Vegas Indoor Skydiving

Every day in Las Vegas, people feel the urge to go skydiving without a parachute. No, they didn't just lose their life's savings at the blackjack tables. They're looking to spend some time at Vegas Indoor Skydiving, the home of one of the biggest adrenaline rushes in town.

Their indoor skydiving facility is the first of its kind in America, built back in 1982. It simulates the freefall experience of skydiving without a plane or a parachute. The freefall effect is created with the use of a vertical wind tunnel powered by a DC3 propeller. It creates winds of up to 120 mph, which is sufficient to support your body weight.

Your experience begins with a short classroom session, where you will learn the proper body positions and flight techniques necessary to have a fun and safe flight. Then it's time to put on your flight suit. The suit is specially vented to catch air. This increases your drag, and gives you more control over your flight. Once your instructor has made sure your suit is ready to go, then you're ready to go – into the wind tunnel, that is.

The instructors are patient and experienced, and yours will accompany you into the wind tunnel. For your first flight, you're definitely going to need him. Until you learn to establish the proper body position, that second pair of hands can help you keep control. The tunnel is heavily padded, so there's no need to fear the occasional mistake.

Your freefall experience will last about three minutes, but it feels a lot longer when you're doing it.

For the sake of comparison, if you had jumped from an actual plane, the freefall time would have been 30-45 seconds.

You can find Vegas Indoor Skydiving near the convention center at the north end of The Strip. Your first flight will cost $75, and a repeat flight on the same day is $40. There's usually a printable $5 off coupon on the site.

What: Vegas Indoor Skydiving

Where: 200 Convention Center Drive

When: 9:45 am-8 pm, daily

What's cool about it: Hovering in mid-air, above a rapidly spinning propeller is pretty much the definition of cool.

Golf

The Las Vegas area offers what is arguably the finest selection of public golf courses in the country. There are over four dozen courses from which to choose. Many of them were designed by big name pros. Here are just a few of the many reasons you'll want to pack your clubs.

Desert Pines Golf Club

With over 4000 mature pine trees, this lovely course was designed by Perry Dye, and inspired by the Pinehurst courses in North Carolina. Water comes into play on half of the holes, and who doesn't love the sight of water in a desert? The extraordinary practice facility is climate-controlled, and features an automatic ball delivery system, so you don't have to bend over to tee up that next practice ball.

Shadow Creek Golf Club

This Tom Fazio designed course is considered the best in town, and one of the best in the world. Each hole is a work of art. Shadow Creek was created as a private course for high rollers only, but a limited number of tee times are available to the public on Mondays through Thursdays. You must be currently staying at an MGM/Mirage property. The steep $500 greens fee includes a round trip limo ride to Shadow Creek and a round on the most luxurious course in town.

Bear's Best

Golfing deity Jack Nicklaus has designed thousands of golf holes on hundreds of courses around the world. Bear's Best is an 18-hole course that duplicates his favorite holes from the various courses. It's a greatest hits collection from one of the heaviest hitters in the game. It's hard to find this kind of variety in a single round of golf anywhere. The nearby Red Rock Mountains form a stunning backdrop for what is sure to be a challenging round.

Tournament Players Club Las Vegas

Take your swing at an actual PGA Tour facility, and enjoy the high standards that are usually reserved for the pros. This Bobby Weed and Raymond Floyd designed course features beautiful views and fast greens. The par 3 greens are islands surrounded by rugged desert. Be accurate or beware!

Paiute Golf Resort

Looking for a good place to play 36 holes? Or 54? Paiute offers you a choice of three championship courses, all designed by Pete Dye. The Snow Mountain and Sun Mountain courses are challenging, but accessible. The Wolf Course is a brute. At 7604 yards, Wolf is the longest course in Nevada, and one of the toughest. At 2800 feet above sea level, Paiute claims to be 8-10 degrees cooler than the other Vegas area courses.

Atomic Testing Museum

From 1951-1962, Las Vegas had a very strange tourist attraction. The city was located only 65 miles from the Nevada Test Site, the nation's top nuclear testing facility. At the appropriate time, gamblers would take a break from their other entertainment so they could go out in the desert and watch a nuclear explosion. Yeah, it kind of makes the Mirage volcano sound puny.

There was a problem with this particular form of entertainment. What happened in Vegas didn't stay in Vegas. Nuclear fallout from the tests would drift wherever the wind took it, ruining the days/weeks/lives of the people who happened to be in its path. This forced a shift to underground testing, which lasted another 30 years.

The 40+ years of above and below ground nuclear testing are meticulously chronicled at the Atomic Testing Museum. The details of the testing facility are covered with a nice mixture of artifacts, reading material, films and interactive displays. The world history of the nuclear age is covered, from the years leading up to the development of the atomic bomb, to the Cold War, to the current day. Pop culture items with a nuclear theme are displayed, and if that gets you hungering for an Atomic Fireball, you'll be happy to know that the candies are for sale in the gift shop.

The highlight of the experience is a 10-minute event that loads the visitors into a bunker and reproduces the look, sound and feel of an atomic explosion (except for that nasty part that includes dying).

The Atomic Testing Museum is located about a mile east of the strip. Admission is $12 for adults. If you're over 65, or aged 7-17, or have a military ID, or have a student ID, then they'll let you in for $9. Kids 6 and under are admitted free, but everything but the 10-minute explosion "ride" will probably bore them. You can plan on at least an hour to see the whole thing, though it could take twice that long if you want to read every word of every display.

What: Atomic Testing Museum

Where: 755 East Flamingo Road

When: Mon-Sat 10 am-5 pm,
Sun 12 pm-5 pm

What's cool about it: Yet another way to visit Las Vegas and get totally bombed.

The Price is Right - Live

If you've ever dreamed of a game show announcer calling your name and screaming "Come on Down!" then you'll want to check out the Bally's version of The Price is Right. There's no Bob Barker, or even Drew Carey, and it won't be broadcast on TV, but a lot of the fun and prizes found in America's longest running game show can be found in this production.

Unlike the television version, where contestants are pre-screened for enthusiasm, nuttiness, and God-knows-what kind of social disorders, The Price is Right Live chooses its contestants randomly. That means you have a chance to get on stage, even if you forgot to paint your face or bring an obnoxious t-shirt.

Once on stage the players bid on prizes and a chance to play one of the traditional Price is Right games, such as Plinko, Cliff Hangers or Hole in One. At one point players get to spin The Big Wheel, and at the end two contestants are chosen to bid on the Showcase. The look of the show is pretty darn authentic, and it should be, since they're using the actual sets from The Price is Right's 35th anniversary season. Beautiful models are on hand to unveil and gesture at each prize, just as in the original show.

There are two frequent hosts of the show: Mark Newton, the host of Hollywood Showdown and Whammy! The All New Press Your Luck on the Game Show Network and Coming Attractions on E!, and David Ruprecht of Supermarket Sweep. While their scripted material can be pretty corny, they both have a good, entertaining rapport with the contestants.

While about 50 people get called for a chance at some sort of prize, that shouldn't be the only reason you go. Your chance of hearing your name is still only about 1 in 6, so the odds are good that you'll be a spectator. The show runs about 105 minutes. While you have to be 21 to be a contestant, guests under 21 are welcome to attend the show as spectators.

A ticket will cost you $56.25.

What: The Price is Right - Live

Where: Bally's Las Vegas, 3645 Las Vegas Boulevard South

When: Tue, Wed, Thur, Sat 2:30 pm, Fri 7:30 pm

What's cool about it: It's the only place that your extensive knowledge of toaster oven prices can help you in Las Vegas.

Nightclubs

You know the kind of glitzy nightclub where everyone dresses to impress and the dance floor is always packed? Where there's a line halfway around the block, and a bouncer guarding the entrance like it was Fort Knox? Most larger cities have one. Las Vegas has a bunch. The ultra-competitive nightclub scene is as large and excessive as anything else in town. You can party like a rock star, or maybe even right next to one, at this selection of the hottest night spots in Vegas.

Tao at the Venetian

Tao has set the Las Vegas nightclub standard for years, and it still attracts its share of celebrities and high-end partygoers. There is stunning Asian décor throughout, culminating in a 20-foot tall mega-Buddha as the centerpiece. There are two very crowded dance floors featuring mostly top-40 mixes. You can also spot some live, nearly-naked women bathing in tubs full of warm water and rose petals. In most places such behavior is unusual, but in Las Vegas it is "decoration."

XS at Encore

Say the name and you've said it all. The 13,000 square foot indoor area spills into a beautiful outdoor pool area for 40,000 square feet of club action. From the gold chandelier, to the gold-plated body molds of lovely female employees, to the VIP booths made from gold-embossed crocodile skin, XS succeeds at excess. They claim to have over 8,000 visitors a night, but only a select few order the $10,000 Dom Perignon cocktail.

Rain at the Palms

They push hard to bring in the celebrities, and the hard work pays off. If you keep your eyes open, you might see someone at least moderately famous. The multi-level club is visually impressive, with state of the art lighting, dancing water fountains, and jets that shoot huge balls of flame. The dance floor is big, and features music that tends toward house or trance.

Marquee at the Cosmopolitan

This 60,000 square foot monster club is like a giant maze, but with seven bars, you can always find a drink. You can choose a laid back party in the Library, a hip hop night in the Boom Box Room, or you can opt for the electric dance music of the main room. The DJs are the stars here. When you're spinning on a 40-foot LED DJ booth surrounded by a three level catwalk filled with dancing girls, that how you know you're the star.

The Bank at Bellagio

As you enter the multi-leveled nightclub known as The Bank, you pass a wall lined with warmly glowing bottles of Cristal. You should take that as a clue that this nightclub is a bit more upscale than the Las Vegas norm. Everyone is dressed sharply, and to get past the ropes, you'll have to do the same. The music is hip hop and top 40, and celebrity DJs are common.

Titanic: The Artifact Exhibition

Whether you loved the movie Titanic or you just like fast-forwarding to the part where Leo DiCaprio dies, the Luxor's Titanic: The Artifact Exhibition is worth a slice of your vacation time. The 25,000 square foot exhibit uses authentic recovered artifacts and detailed reproductions to tell the story of the doomed ocean liner.

At the beginning of your tour, you will receive a boarding pass containing the name, age and itinerary of an actual Titanic passenger. When the tour completes, you get a chance to check out the wall memorial to see if your passenger was one of the 705 survivors or one of the over 1500 who went down with the ship. It's a creepy but effective way to immerse you in the experience.

The recovered artifacts vary from the mundane (pieces of luggage, floor tiles from the first class smoking room) to luxurious (sparkling jewelry pieces, an unopened bottle of 1900 vintage champagne), and are presented in a manner that tells a detailed story of the shipboard experience for the passengers and crew. There is also "The Big Piece" – the largest Titanic artifact ever retrieved. It is merely a 26-foot-long piece of the ship's hull that weighs in at 15 tons!

While the real artifacts are quite impressive, this is Las Vegas, so the fake stuff is really cool too. The cabins have been re-created using furnishings from the original manufacturers. While the first class cabins are pretty nice, the third class cabins are a claustrophobe's nightmare. There's a full-sized reproduction of the Grand Staircase and a reproduced Promenade Deck that is chilling... literally. They keep it cooled to approximate the weather conditions on that fateful night.

The exhibit is self-guided, so you can go at your own pace. Allot an hour and you won't miss by much. It'll cost you $28 as an adult, $26 for seniors, or $21 for children 4-12.

What: Titanic: The Artifact Exhibition

Where: Luxor Hotel and Casino, 3900 Las Vegas Boulevard South

When: 10 am-10 pm, daily

What's cool about it: It's the only disaster in town bigger than Criss Angel's show.

Showcase Mall

The Showcase Mall is less a mall than a collection of interesting and unique places. It's only half a block from MGM Grand on the south end of The Strip, so it's worth stopping in. It's the place with the gigantic Coca Cola bottle at the front. If someone refers to the "Coca Cola Mall," this is the place they're talking about. The mall has three main attractions.

First, there's M&M's World, which is a four-floor tribute to the chocolate that melts in your mouth but not in your hand. You'll see Kyle Busch's #18 NASCAR stock car. You can shop thousands of M&M-themed souvenirs, from t-shirts to toys to shiny stuff made of Swarovski crystal. You can also view, "I Lost My M in Las Vegas," a funny little 3-D film with free admission. Oh yeah, there's also chocolate. You can build your own bag of M&M's from their selection of 22 colors. Want a bag with only green ones? Want to mix regular and peanut? You can do it. It's total anarchy!

The World of Coca Cola is a similar place, but on a smaller scale. There's some Coke memorabilia and an old fashioned soda fountain that will sell you a Coke ice cream float. You can also purchase the 16 flavors of Coke package that allows you to taste the various versions of Coke that are sold around the world. Be careful, though. If you get hooked on the Italian version of Coke, that can be a pretty expensive addiction.

The last big attraction is GameWorks; a giant arcade. Dance games. Motion games. Ticket games. Crane games. And good old video games. You can pay on a per game basis, or buy a pass that lets you play all you want for an hourly charge.

There is some good old-fashioned mall stuff here too. You can get your Starbucks fix at the food court or check your email at an internet café. Grab a movie at the eight-screen theater or pick up discount show tickets at Tix 4 Tonight.

What: Showcase Mall

Where: 3785 Las Vegas Boulevard South

When: (M&M's World) 9am-midnight, daily, other tenants vary

What's cool about it: M&M's and Coke. Sugar rush!

The Gun Store

If your idea of stress relief is pulling out a gun and blowing holes in things, then you have to be very careful about where you choose to relieve your stress. That sort of thing is frowned upon in most of the country. Heck, even in most of Las Vegas.

You're in luck, though. The folks at The Gun Store have just the right combination of firepower and fantasy to relieve your violent urges. The Gun Store is a full-service shooting range, with a high-quality facility and numerous licensed instructors, but their specialty is something that many seasoned gun handlers have never had the opportunity to try – they give you the chance to fire a machine gun.

There are dozens of guns to choose from, and some entertaining package deals that provide a variety of shooting experiences. Fans of the film "Zombieland" will enjoy the Zombie Package. They set up the zombie targets, and you fill 'em full of lead (or, environmentally friendly lead-free ammo, at least). Blast away with a shotgun and a 1911 pistol. If that doesn't send the walking dead running, follow up with an HK33 assault rifle, and finish them off with 50 shots from an UZI submachine gun. Don't forget the double tap!

The instructors know that many of their customers have never fired a gun before, and they've got the patience necessary to walk you through it. They're also experienced enough to recognize a shooter who knows what he's doing. Once you show yourself as such a shooter, they won't smother you with unnecessary instruction.

Cost of ammunition is the main price factor. The more you shoot, the more you pay. The various packages start at $40 (the Kids Package) and work their way up from there. The Shoot in the Dark package lets you do just that, complete with laser sighting and night vision goggles for $200. The Shoot the Wall package gives you a chance to fire twelve different machine guns for $399.95.

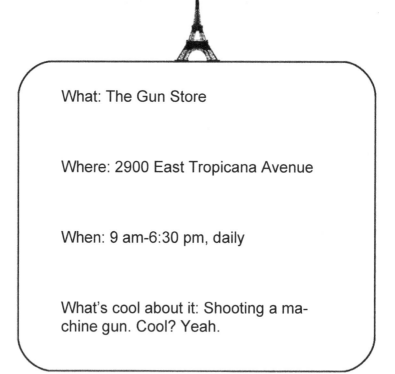

What: The Gun Store

Where: 2900 East Tropicana Avenue

When: 9 am-6:30 pm, daily

What's cool about it: Shooting a machine gun. Cool? Yeah.

Day Spas

Las Vegas is absolutely brimming with world class spas. The variety of treatments available is staggering. Whether you're looking for a simple massage or an all-day pampering, these places will treat you right.

Qua Baths and Spa – Caesars Palace

Enjoy up to three Roman baths (hot, cold or tepid). Relax in the Laconium, a soothing sauna that is kept at 140 degrees. If cold more to your liking, try out the Arctic Room, where flakes of snow fall from the ceiling and melt on your skin. There's also a tea room with its own tea sommelier, who will pair tea to your various treatments the same way a restaurant sommelier would pair wine with gourmet food.

The Spa – Wynn Las Vegas

Relax in their eucalyptus steam room, or just stand in the awesome deluge shower, which simulates a cleansing waterfall. There's a full menu of treatments available, but a Las Vegas favorite is the Good Luck Ritual. The treatment is based upon the five Chinese elements, and is designed to promote happiness, prosperity, and, of course, luck. The combination of custom massage, foot treatment, hand treatment and scalp therapy may not make you luckier, but it does promote happiness.

the bathhouse – THEhotel at Mandalay Bay

Stylish elegance is the trademark of THEhotel, and their bathhouse spa fits right in. Its slate and marble décor just screams "trendy," or rather, whispers it softly. Try their signature Scents-of-you-Massage, a warm stone massage featuring an individualized mix of aromatherapy oils specially formulated to suit your style (based upon a short questionnaire you fill out upon arrival).

Spa Bellagio – The Bellagio

This large, beautiful facility offers a wide variety of treatments, but their innovative massage therapies are the most popular. The Watsu Massage is a combination of Zen Shiatsu and stretching, while floating in a tranquil, 94-degree pool. The Ashiatsu Oriental Bar Therapy is an ancient form of bodywork that uses deep compression techniques. The barefoot therapist hangs from bars attached to the ceiling, performing the massage with her feet.

The Spa – Aria

This two-level spa has its massive fitness center on a different floor from the spa treatments, so you can keep your work and your relaxation separate. In addition to the expected collection of treatments and massages, The Spa at Aria is the only place in the U.S. that offers Japanese Ganbanyoku beds. These heated stone beds are reputed to accelerate metabolism, increase circulation, and eliminate toxins from the body.

CSI: The Experience

Las Vegas is the setting of the longtime television hit CSI. The MGM Grand is the home of CSI: The Experience, an interactive exhibit that casts you in the role of crime solver. You investigate the crime scene. You gather the evidence. You submit your results to Gil Grissom (for non-CSI watchers, he's your boss).

As the experience begins, you get your choice of three different crime scenes. At this point, and at various points during the experience, you'll receive a video briefing from CSI cast members. After you make your choice, you get an opportunity to visit your crime scene and take notes of the details you observe. Then it's off to the lab, where you get a look at the evidence collected from your scene.

The lab is the highlight of the experience. The various cases might have you dealing with microscopes, DNA systems, computer databases, ballistics identification systems, chemistry equipment and reagents, and UV light sources. There are video presentations from real world scientists that explain what you're doing and why you're doing it.

Once you process all of your evidence, an interactive touch screen allows you to submit your findings and tell Gil who dunnit. If you are correct, Gil will ration you a measured teaspoon of fatherly praise. Otherwise, he informs you that you are being exiled to CSI: Detroit.

You are allowed to visit the various stations and solve the crime at your own pace. Most people take an hour, give or take 15 minutes. The three crime scenes are unique, so if you come back and do another one it's a new experience (for a new admission price).

Admission is $30 for adults or $23 for kids 4-11. If you really want junior to get the autopsy report from Doc Robbins, just remember that children under 12 must be accompanied by an adult. Coupons for $5 off the admission price are common online and around town.

What: CSI: The Experience

Where: MGM Grand Hotel and Casino, 3799 Las Vegas Boulevard South

When: 9 am-9 pm, daily

What's cool about it: Reporting your results to Gil Grissom. Oh, the pressure!

Pinball Hall of Fame

When you visit Las Vegas, you're sure to see plenty of bright colors and flashing lights. Not all of that activity is limited to the casinos. Just a few blocks from The Strip, you'll find a place where coins are dropping and machines are chirping, but nobody is gambling.

You'll find the Pinball Hall of Fame in a large, plain building on Tropicana Avenue. The interior isn't fancy, but it is focused on its theme – pinball machines. There are hundreds of them, along with a nice selection of classic video games, all laid out in neat rows. There is no admission charge. Just walk in and take a look around.

Each machine is a work of art collected from the various eras of pinball history. From the simple tables of the 1950s, through the golden age of the 70s and 80s, to the flashy machines of the 21st century, the Pinball Hall of Fame feels like a museum dedicated to the pursuit of the silver ball. It's better than that, though. What kind of museum lets you play with the art? They don't just display 'em, they let you play 'em.

All of the machines are available to be played. Some will cost you a single quarter. Some more recent games go for fifty or seventy-five cents. At those prices, the PHoF might qualify as the best entertainment value in town.

Beyond the obvious rarity, the average 30-40 year old pinball machine has another problem. When you find one, it hardly ever works right. It's probably in a bar or a restaurant where the owner has no clue how to maintain it. That isn't a problem here. Pinball machines are notorious for breaking, but there's someone working pretty much constantly to keep the machines running.

It costs a little extra to keep the games in top working order, but the Pinball Hall of Fame isn't about the money (shhh, don't tell the rest of Vegas). In fact, they're a registered not-for-profit corporation. Many of your extra quarters will eventually find their way to the Salvation Army.

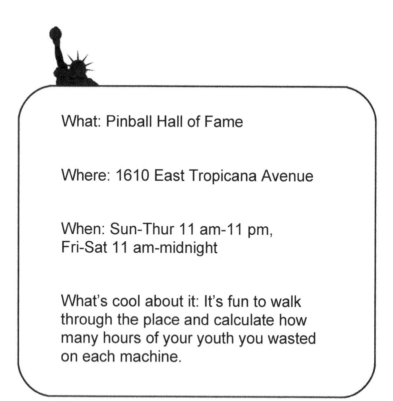

What: Pinball Hall of Fame

Where: 1610 East Tropicana Avenue

When: Sun-Thur 11 am-11 pm,
Fri-Sat 11 am-midnight

What's cool about it: It's fun to walk through the place and calculate how many hours of your youth you wasted on each machine.

Fast Lap Indoor Kart Racing

We've all seen those go-cart places where you putter around the track in a cart that feels like it was powered by AAA batteries. Fast Lap Indoor Kart Racing is not such a place. Once you pay your money and sign your waiver, they'll put you in a gas powered cart with a 200cc Honda engine. Put your foot down and that thing will move (up to 50 mph).

As part of your preparation you are shown a short video on driving instructions and course rules. You suit up in a helmet, gloves, head sock, and a racing jumpsuit. The jumpsuit is cool to look at but hot to wear. Wearing it isn't mandatory, so it's your call.

The duration of a race is based on time. Weekend races are 10-minutes long. That's generally enough time to run 17-21 laps around the nine-turn track. The sessions on Monday through Friday are 12-minutes long. At the end of your race you'll get a printout of your various lap times and the lap times of the people who raced with you. If you purchase multiple races, you'll be able to see yourself improve as a driver. Another thing will happen at the end of your race; you'll probably be exhausted. Getting around this track 20 times is an adrenaline rush, but it can take the wind out of you.

The standard price for a single race is $25. They frequently hand out coupons on the strip that will get you three races for $45. It's also worth checking out the specials on their website at fastlaplv.com.

This is not an activity for young kids. You've got to be five feet tall to drive one of the cars, and if you're under 18 you must be accompanied by an adult.

If you have a group of 8 or larger you can get a special rate. They do lots of corporate events too. Just give them a call and set it up in advance. They'll even come pick you and your group up.

What: Fast Lap Indoor Kart Racing

Where: 4288 S. Polaris #109

When: Mon-Sat 11am-11 pm,
Sun 11 am-9 pm

What's cool about it: The head sock.
Chicks dig the head sock.

Helicopter Tours

Some of the sights in and around Las Vegas are best seen from the air, and there are plenty of helicopter tour companies to get you off the ground. Although there are a wide variety of tour options, two of them are by far the most popular.

The helicopter tour of The Strip is always a favorite. Usually best done at night, these flights whisk you into the sky for a whirlwind tour above the coolest place in the world. There's usually a champagne toast before takeoff, and then it's up, up and away. The observation tower at the Stratosphere can get you this high into the air, but it can only give you one angle of The Strip. The helicopter ride offers a variety of viewing angles. It's definitely a better way to view South Strip. The flight is relatively quick (around 12 minutes), but the experience is unforgettable. Most tours allow photography, but night film is recommended.

The Grand Canyon tour is the king of helicopter tours. First of all, we're talking air-conditioned helicopters. Roasting 1000 feet above the desert floor is nobody's idea of a vacation. Most tours include a scenic pass over the Hoover Dam and Lake Mead, and an excellent view of the Grand Canyon and everything on the way. The pilots tend to be friendly and knowledgeable, and most will happily field questions. Flights go into the Grand Canyon itself and land you on the canyon floor. There's usually about 30 minutes of walking around time, and perhaps a light meal. There's often a quick buzz over The Strip when you get back to town. If you figure four hours for the entire trip you won't be far wrong.

Some of the more popular tour companies are look! tours (looktours.com), Papillon (papillon.com), Maverick (maverickhelicopter.com) and Adventure Helicopter Tours (adventurehelicoptertours.com).

The prices and services from the various helicopter tour companies vary widely, so it's worth shopping around. Some will pick you up at your hotel in a limo, and others expect you to show up at their flight point. It pays to read the fine print and see what is included in any package. Speaking of fine print, there are also fuel surcharges that are not always included in the advertised prices.

Bellagio Gallery of Fine Art

When Steve Wynn opened the Bellagio in 1998, it included an art gallery. There were plenty of naysayers who said that visitors wouldn't take time from their Las Vegas debauchery for such a cultured activity. The gallery defied those predictions by attracting large crowds. Those crowds, however, had come to see pieces predominately from Wynn's fabulous personal collection. When Wynn sold the Bellagio in 2000, and took his personal art collection with him, the future of the gallery was in doubt. How could it operate successfully without Wynn's permanent collection?

The answer can be found in the current version of the Bellagio Gallery of Fine Art. It has attracted a series of high quality exhibits to replace its resident collection. The gallery now bills itself as the place "where great art goes on vacation." Exhibits stay on display for a number of months, and are then replaced by something completely different.

After a few years of operating in this format, they have developed an impressive track record. Each exhibit features high quality work by big name artists. The shows tend to be relatively compact (25-30 pieces) and well-focused on their respective themes. The "Figuratively Speaking" show, which celebrated the human form with works by Renoir, Picasso and others, was replaced by "A Sense of Place: Landscapes from Monet to Hockney" in mid-2011.

When you attend, you will receive an audio wand with your admission. It allows you to hear a detailed description of each work. If you prefer the personal touch, an experienced museum professional conducts a 45-minute tour at 2:00 p.m. daily.

The Bellagio Gallery is one of those places that remind you of a blunt fact about Las Vegas – it's expensive. Adult admission is $15, which, depending on the exchange rate, is a little more than you would pay to enter The Louvre in Paris (that's Paris, France, not Paris Las Vegas). Seniors can get in for $12, and a student, teacher or military ID will get you $10 admission.

What: Bellagio Gallery of Fine Art

Where: Bellagio, 3600 Las Vegas Boulevard South

When: Wed, Fri, Sat 10 am-7 pm, Sun, Mon, Tue, Thur 10 am-6 pm

What's cool about it: The changing exhibits. You can see different art each time you deliver.

Venetian Gondola Rides

If you're looking for a break from the fast pace of Vegas, a relaxing ride in an authentic wooden gondola might be just what you need. The Venetian offers two versions of their iconic ride, each one with a different course and different sights.

The gondoliers look like the real thing, with black and white striped shirts, straw hats and red scarves. Some are actually from Italy, and many can speak and sing in Italian.

The indoor version of the ride can be found in the Grand Canal Shoppes, The Venetian's extraordinary shopping mall. Your half-mile trip will take you down the fantastic indoor canal, winding your way under bridges and past the various shops. Your gondolier will sing to you as you drift beneath the blue-painted sky and marvel at the detailed, Italian-themed design of the Canal Shoppes.

The outdoor version can be found right in front of The Venetian, in the enormous man-made lagoon. Being outdoors in the elements makes the gondola ride feel more like the real thing (though bad weather can occasionally close the outdoor ride down for the day). A slow ride around the lagoon is the perfect opportunity to marvel at the soaring architecture of The Venetian itself.

A nighttime gondola ride can be very romantic, but it's significantly less so when you're staring across the boat at a couple of strangers. The gondolas are designed to seat four, so sharing is the norm. If you show up at an off time, you might luck into a gondola for two. You can make your own luck with cash, as a private ride is one of the purchasable options when you buy your tickets.

Want to get married on a gondola? The Venetian knew that you would, so they have created a shining, white and gold gondola for your special day. It has room for all of the wedding essentials: a bride, a groom, a minister, a witness... and a gondolier.

Show up at 9:45 a.m. or 4:15 p.m. to see the beginning or end of the shift. The costumed gondoliers march through the Canal Shoppes in single file, singing Italian songs.

What: Venetian Gondola Rides

Where: The Venetian Resort Hotel Casino, 3355 Las Vegas Blvd. South

When: (Indoor) Sun-Thur 10 am-11 pm, Fri-Sat 10 am-midnight
(Outdoor) 12 pm-11 pm

What's cool about it: Doing your own amateur translation of the songs the gondoliers sing.

Pools

When you stay at a nice resort, you expect a nice swimming pool. That's just the way it is in most places. That isn't enough for Las Vegas, though. Extravagant luxury pools are the norm here. Some pools have even become party destinations, with music provided by famous recording artist or celebrity DJs. Meet, greet and beat the heat with this selection of the top pools in town.

"Fun in the Sun Pools"

Mandalay Bay

When it comes to pool areas, Mandalay Bay Beach is the king of the beach. The eleven acre complex offers three swimming pools and an actual beach with 2,700 tons of real sand. Go for a run on the jogging track, enjoy the ups and downs of the wave pool, or slowly navigate your way around the lazy river. Add in a couple of restaurants, a couple of bars, and over 100 cabanas, and you've got a pretty sweet way to spend an afternoon.

Flamingo

The Flamingo's beautiful fifteen acre pool area is a tropical oasis in the desert. Among the waterfalls and palm trees, you'll find four pools, a poolside bar, a beach shop, and a restaurant. A series of waterslides crisscross the area. Pink flamingo fountains send water arching into the pool. If you prefer the real thing, actual pink flamingos live nearby, in the wildlife refuge.

Golden Nugget

What it lacks in size, the Golden Nugget pool area makes up for in sheer coolness. Smack dab in the middle of the pool is something every pool needs – a shark tank! Swim right up and say hello to five species of sharks and a couple of hundred fish. There's also a three-story waterslide that twists around the pool area and carries you right through the center of the shark habitat. You should see the looks on the sharks' faces as they watch you go zipping by.

MGM Grand

MGM's massive Grand Pool Complex offers five swimming pools, three whirlpools, and a very long lazy river that will take you almost ten minutes to traverse. This is prime relaxation real estate. One pool is just a couple of inches deep, and lined with partially-submerged lounge chairs. There are also plenty of shady areas, so you can snooze without roasting.

Caesars Palace

Caesars Palace offers a huge, sprawling complex with multiple named pools, so you're certain to find one to your liking. The Apollo pool has the best sun expo-sure. The Neptune pool is ideally sized for swimming laps. The Fortuna pool offers swim-up blackjack, and a lounge with a scotch tasting menu. The Venus pool is an adults-only pool club with a DJ and topless tanning.

"Party Pools"

Hard Rock

The Hard Rock pool is a party pool. It's loud, and populated by the beautiful and/or famous. Their Sunday Rehab party is a legendary, all-day party, with a couple of thousand attendees. Most of them are half-clothed and at least half-drunk. Expect to stand in line and pay a steep cover charge.

Encore

Encore Beach Club isn't as large as some of the other party pools in town, but what it lacks in size, it makes up in style. It boasts one of the most beautiful facilities in town. The outrageous, air conditioned cabanas and bungalows attract the rich and famous. Think of it as a classy night club where you can't use clothing to hide your flaws. Intimidating? For most of us, yeah.

Palms

The pool at the Palms is the outdoor party place of choice for the young and trendy. Their summer Ditch Fridays parties get the weekend started right. Their frequent evening pool parties feature live music and superstar DJs. The Palms' affiliation with the Playboy Club frequently pays dividends in the form of Playboy bunnies catching some rays.

CBS Television City Research Center

Sometimes we watch television and ask ourselves a simple question: How did this junk get on the air? Part of the answer can be found at the MGM Grand, at the CBS Television City research center. In exchange for just a little bit of your time, you can mold the future of television – or at least the portion of television that appears on CBS, MTV, VH1, Nickelodeon, and the other Viacom networks.

Once you grab your free ticket, you will be asked to show up for one of the sessions that begin every half hour. You will get the opportunity to watch a pilot for an upcoming show.

When the show is over, you will use a touch screen to answer a series of questions. You might get a chance to see something really good, or you might see something that will make you beg them please, please, for the sake of humanity, do not put this on the air. Give them your honest opinion. If the show sucks, they want you to tell them.

The entire process is pretty quick and very low-pressure. Expect to spend between 45-90 minutes, depending on the length of the show. At the end, you get an envelope with a handful of nice coupons for MGM Grand restaurants and attractions.

The Sony 3D Experience is also here, so you might get a chance to give your opinion of some of their new home theater electronics items.

In either case, there's a small chance that you will be asked to participate in a session that features a live interview. The lucky and cooperative few are sometimes rewarded with more than coupons – a little bit of cash ($75-100)!

Before and after your session, you'll have a chance to browse a gift shop offering merchandise from the various television networks. If you see something you like, wait until after your session to buy it, since your envelope of coupons might help with the price.

It takes a bit of searching to find the research center. It's all the way at the end of the Studio Walk, near the pool. Feel free to bring the kids, since children 10 and older are welcome.

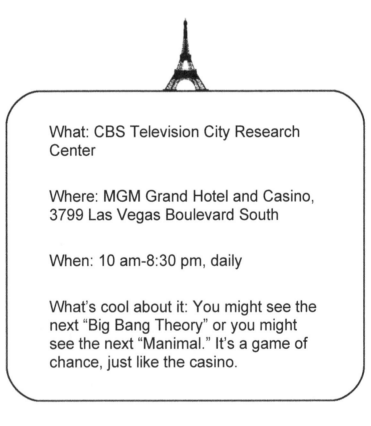

What: CBS Television City Research Center

Where: MGM Grand Hotel and Casino, 3799 Las Vegas Boulevard South

When: 10 am-8:30 pm, daily

What's cool about it: You might see the next "Big Bang Theory" or you might see the next "Manimal." It's a game of chance, just like the casino.

Exotics Racing

If you dream of racing around a track in a car that costs more than most people's homes, then Exotics Racing is for you. From their location at the Las Vegas Motor Speedway, the folks at Exotics have a large fleet of supercars just waiting for you to drive them.

If you always wanted to drive a Porsche, then this is your chance. You can roll like James Bond behind the wheel of an Aston Martin V8 Vantage. If you're looking for a taste of Italy, perhaps you would enjoy one of their Ferrari or Lamborghini offerings. The Lamborghini Murcielago LP640 is a V12 beast that'll take you from 0-60 in 3.3 seconds. If you like that sort of thing.

Once you choose the car of your dreams, here's how it works. You'll begin with some classroom instruction. An instructor will fill you in on the proper driving position, steering technique, and the braking and acceleration tendencies of powerful cars. You'll also get some info on your specific car. Then it's out to the race track for two discovery laps in a Hummer H2. An instructor will drive you around the track and show you what you're getting yourself into.

Then it's the moment you've been waiting for. You slip behind the wheel of your chosen supercar and take it for a spin. There's a driving instructor in the passenger seat charged with making sure you take full advantage of your machine's abilities, but do so within the realms of safety. That means he'll keep you off the wall, but he'll also tell you to put your foot down, if you're driving like a wimp.

The basic package includes five laps around the track, but more laps can be purchased. The basic packages start at $199 for the Porsche and go to $399 for the top end Ferraris or Lamborghinis. When you get into extra laps and multi-car packages the sky's the limit.

What: Exotics Racing

Where: Las Vegas Motor Speedway, 7000 Las Vegas Boulevard North

When: Track dates vary, but Tue, Wed, Fri and Sat are the most common.

What's cool about it: Putting the accelerator all the way to the floor in a car where that means something.

Siegfried & Roy's Secret Garden and Dolphin Habitat

Siegfried and Roy's hugely popular stage show ended in 2003, but their Secret Garden and Dolphin Habitat live on at The Mirage.

The Secret Garden is basically a zoo. It isn't a huge zoo, but it has plenty of big cats – the animals that are the stars of major zoos. There are lions, golden tigers, black panthers and leopards. Most notably, Siegfried and Roy have a large collection of extremely rare white lions and white tigers. Depending on when you visit, you might get to see them feed a white tiger cub, which is one of the most ridiculously cute things you will ever witness.

Did you know that black panthers are actually leopards? That's just one of the things you'll learn as you view the big cats (Well, you just read it here, so you can't learn it there. But you understand.). Numerous trainers are on hand at the exhibit to answer your questions and dispense little bits of knowledge like this. As Bill Cosby said, "If you're not careful, you might learn something before it's done."

The Dolphin Habitat is home to a family of Atlantic bottlenose dolphins. With the 2008 birth of a calf named Bella, there are now three generations of dolphins at the Habitat. They don't force the dolphins to do tricks, but if you toss them a beach ball they'll bop it back at you, because that's what dolphins like to do. Again, numerous trainers are present to educate you on all things dolphiny.

If you can't get enough of the aquatic mammals, you might want to consider the Trainer for a Day program. This is more than just tossing on a wetsuit and swimming with the dolphins. This is an all-day event (10 a.m. – 4 p.m.) where you get a chance to train, play with, swim with and feed the dolphins. The price is steep, but the coolness factor is high.

Admission to the Secret Garden and Dolphin Habitat is $17 for adults and $12 for children 4-12. They knock a few bucks off the price if you're staying at the Mirage. The Trainer for a Day program is $595.

What: Siegfried & Roy's Secret Garden and Dolphin Habitat

Where: The Mirage, 3400 Las Vegas Boulevard South

When: Mon-Fri 11 am-6 pm, weekends and holidays 10 am-6 pm

What's cool about it: Dolphins *are* entertainment.

Gentlemen's Clubs

You don't get the nickname Sin City without offering up your fair share of sin. For those seeking adult entertainment, Las Vegas offers the finest selection of strip clubs in the world. No bachelor party in Vegas would be complete without a visit to one of these world-famous clubs.

Sapphire Gentleman's Club

At over 70,000 square feet, Sapphire is the world's largest strip club. It's just enormous. There are 400 girls performing nightly, so you're surrounded by them at all times. You can't turn your head without seeing one. It's like being in a music video. If you believe that there's no bad time to go to a strip club, then Sapphire is the place for you. They're open 24/7/365. Merry Christmas!

Palomino Club

Las Vegas has a rule for strip clubs. If your strippers are totally nude, you cannot serve alcohol. Because of this, most clubs choose to limit their girls to toplessness, so they can cash in on the alcohol. The Palomino club is the exception to this rule. They've been there since 1969, so they were grandfathered in on the old rule set. If you want totally nude dancers, and want to enjoy a full bar while you watch them, this is the only place in town.

Olympic Garden Gentlemen's Club

OG bills itself as the only strip club on The Strip. Two blocks north of the Stratosphere may not meet your definition of The Strip, but at least it's close. This is a two-level club, with women dancing downstairs and men dancing upstairs. They've often got bachelor and bachelorette parties running at the same time, sometimes from the same wedding party!

Treasures Gentlemen's Club & Steakhouse

Yes. That's right. They have a steakhouse. You might be surprised to find out that it's actually a pretty good one. That doesn't mean they skimp on the strip club, though. There are lots of girls in a classy environment. Grab a package deal that includes a limousine ride, dinner, and a VIP table in the strip club. It'll save you a bundle.

Spearmint Rhino

This is the most popular club in town, and considered one of the best in the world. They feature hundreds of beautiful women every day. Couples are welcome, and treated quite well. Call in advance and they'll pick you up at any hotel in town. Not only is the ride free, but when you arrive this way, you'll pay no cover charge! Getting home is your responsibility, but taxis are plentiful.

Bodies... The Exhibition

Now that the mob no longer runs Las Vegas, your best chance to see a dead body when you come to town is at Bodies... The Exhibition at the Luxor. This is a presentation of actual dead human bodies, and while such a thing might not be at the top of your vacation to-do list, the result is memorable, educational and surprisingly tasteful.

Various human bodies are displayed either in full or as dissected organs, offering views rarely seen by anyone outside of the medical profession. Virtually every part of the human body is displayed and every system is explained (muscular, nervous, circulatory, etc...). Healthy bodies and organs are compared and contrasted with examples of bodies with diseases. For instance, you can see the stark difference between a healthy lung and a smoker's lung.

There is a separate section that shows various stages of fetal development, including some birth defects. Some people find this section upsetting, so it is clearly marked for the benefit of those who prefer to avoid it.

There is a definite shock associated with the viewing of actual dead human bodies, but when the shock passes, you're left with a far more enduring educational experience than you could have found in a textbook.

The science behind the exhibition is a story unto itself. The bodies and organs are preserved using a polymer preservation process, which basically allows them to be displayed forever. This process is explained in as much detail as you desire.

Admission is $32 for adults and $24 for children. Children are encouraged to attend, but only with adult supervision. You can be the judge of whether your kids will find it educational or just nightmare-inducing.

What: Bodies... The Exhibition

Where: Luxor Hotel and Casino, 3900 Las Vegas Boulevard South

When: 10 am-10 pm, daily

What's cool about it: No matter how wrecked you are from last night's partying, you're still doing better than these bodies.

Stripper 101

There are two types of women who attend the popular Stripper 101 class at Planet Hollywood – those who think that a class on stripping and pole dancing sounds like a hoot, and those who are kind of nervous and self conscious about the whole thing. The first group ends up enjoying the class. The second group usually enjoys it even more.

The class is taught on a dimly-lit stage that simulates the conditions in a gentlemen's club. Your instructor will demonstrate a number of simple but effective pole dancing maneuvers that are used by professional dancers. You will then get a chance to try out the moves yourself, on one of the many poles available for students. You'll also learn the techniques of the big moneymaker – the lap dance.

One of the themes of the Stripper 101 class is learning to lose your inhibitions, so every class package includes a cocktail to get thing started. From that point on, it's easy to relax and have fun with the experience. There's no nudity, from either the instructor or the students. The classes consist of all women. No exceptions. You can dress as slutty or comfortably as you like, and you won't have to worry about strange guys leering at you. You even get to try out your lap dance techniques on an empty chair. It's a comfortable afternoon with the girls.

The class is designed for women of all ages, shapes and sizes. The techniques are pretty basic. You're not going to end up hanging upside down on the pole.

Your instructor might, though. Each class is taught by an actual Las Vegas exotic dancer, and some of them are quite limber. The 75 minute class is a bit of a workout. It's nothing drop-dead exhausting, but you will use a few muscles you don't normally flex.

At the end, you will receive your official stripper license, filled out with your chosen "stripper name." Pictures are taken at the beginning of the class, and available for purchase at the end. You can even buy your own stripper pole, in case you want to practice your newfound skills on someone special.

Packages range from $39.99 - $79.99. They do a big business in bachelorette parties and girls' nights out. Groups of eight or more can get a group discount.

What: Stripper 101

Where: Planet Hollywood V Theater, 3667 Las Vegas Boulevard South

When: Sun-Thur 3 pm, 4:30 pm/ Fri 3 pm, 4:30 pm, 6 pm/Sat 11:30 am, 1 pm, 3 pm, 4:30 pm, 6 pm

What's cool about it: Learn fallback skills in case the economy gets worse.

Stratosphere Thrill Rides and Observation Deck

If you're on The Strip and you look north, that 1149-foot-tall pointy thing is the Stratosphere. The Stratosphere is the tallest building in Las Vegas and the tallest observation tower in the United States. Some very interesting options are available to those willing to make the trek into the sky.

The most basic activity is the observation deck. It features a 360° view of the city from both indoor and outdoor vantage points. Since the sky is usually very clear out in the desert, you can see for miles. For a surreal experience, visit on the Fourth of July, and watch the various Las Vegas fireworks shows in town – from above. A bar is available, offering "liquid courage" to those in need. If you're planning to ride one of the thrill rides, a stop at the bar might sound pretty good.

There are four rides available at the top of the tower, and none are for the faint of heart. The first ride goes by the unassuming name of Insanity. A mechanical arm extends 64 feet from the side of the building and commences spinning you around. Think of one of those octopus rides at the fair, only 900 feet in the air and spinning at three Gs.

The Big Shot is the world's highest thrill ride. It fires you and your fellow passengers straight up the mast of the tower, to a maximum height of 1081 feet. It takes about two seconds for your high speed journey up the mast. Then, just as you're about to recover from the sudden acceleration, it drops you.

The X-Scream is probably the tamest of the choices up here. You're on a giant teeter-totter, dangling over the edge of the Strat, head-first, 866 feet above the ground. It's still not for the wimpy.

If you like simplicity in your thrill rides, it's tough to beat the Sky Jump. You take an elevator to the top of a towering building, walk up to the edge, and jump off. That's right. You jump off the edge of the Stratosphere. It's actually quite a bit more complicated than that. It's a controlled free fall off the 108th floor. Numerous precautions are taken to make sure you don't go splat. Control of your bodily functions is up to you.

Expect to pay $16 just to get up to the Observation Deck, and another $12-13 per ride ($99 for the Sky Jump). You can save on package deals. For $34 you get a trip to the Ob Deck and all the X-Scream, Big Shot and Insanity you can eat. It's a huge deal.

What: Stratosphere Thrill Rides and Observation Deck

Where: The Stratosphere, 2000 Las Vegas Boulevard

When: Sun-Thur 11am-1 am, Fri-Sat 11 am-2 am

What's cool about it: The bar. After a few drinks, none of the rides look all that scary.

Weddings

Yes, people do still get married, especially in Las Vegas. Over 100,000 couples do it each year, and that doesn't even count those choosing to renew their vows! No other city in the world offers the variety of wedding options you can find in Las Vegas. When you tie the knot here, you'll be joining some good company (Sinatra, Elvis, Angelina Jolie). From the elegant to the unusual, this is how you find marital bliss the Vegas way.

Bellagio

The Bellagio opened in 1998, at a cost of $1.6 billion, and that was back in the days when a billion dollars was a lot of money. It is still one of the most elegant places in town. In their two beautiful chapels, they offer wedding packages starting at $1500. It is the most popular marriage destination of all The Strip hotels.

A Little White Wedding Chapel

Plenty of celebrities like this famous chapel. Mary Tyler Moore and Michael Jordan got married here. No, not to each other. They offer you a choice of five different wedding chapels. If you're running late for a show or a dinner reservation, you can opt for a drive-thru wedding in a limo or other vehicle of your choice. Out-of-town friends can view your special event on the chapel's webcam.

Chapel of the Bells

You might have seen this small, pretty chapel in any of a variety of movies ("Indecent Proposal", "Vegas Vacation", "Honeymoon in Vegas"). You can find the world famous Chapel of the Bells at the north end of The Strip. Wedding packages start at $135. It's a very popular combination of value and convenience.

Caesars Palace

At Caesars they ask, "Why get married at a chapel when you can get married at a Palace?" Whether your needs are majestic or intimate, Caesars has something for you. They offer three beautiful indoor chapels and two absolutely stunning outdoor venues. Packages start at $850, and weekend rates are higher.

Unusual Weddings

The various hotels on The Strip offer some unusual places to exchange your vows. The Venetian will let marry you in a gondola. Paris offers a ceremony at the top of their Eiffel Tower. New York New York will do it on a roller coaster at 67 mph. With a little advance warning, you can find an Elvis impersonator to marry you on virtually any square inch of Las Vegas soil.

The Roller Coaster at New York New York

You're 100% sure you're in Las Vegas. But if you walk into a place that looks like a New York subway station and get into a car that looks like a New York taxi cab, then you have just boarded the roller coaster at New York New York.

This Coney Island style coaster ride times out at just under 3 minutes, which is a pretty good length. It might not be the scariest coaster you've ever ridden, but it has some nice features. In addition to a couple of corkscrews and inversion loops, there's a 144 foot drop and a maximum speed of 67 mph. Prepare to get bumped around a bit, because the ride is not always smooth.

The best segment of the trip is the part that takes place outdoors. You not only get an excellent view of the resort's New York landscape (complete with Statue of Liberty, Empire State Building and New York Harbor), but you actually become a part of it as your car zips among the monuments. You'll be that tiny screaming dot in the background of various peoples' vacation pictures. You also get some stunning views of The Strip. The view is always pretty sweet, but it looks even better when you ride at night.

Before or after your ride, take a walk through the giant Coney Island Emporium, complete with carnival games, laser tag, and over 200 coin operated video games. It's one of the best arcades in town.

The arcade and the roller coaster entrance are on the second floor of the New York New York property. It'll cost you $14 to ride, but an all-day pass is only $25. They'll snap your picture as you ride, and offer to sell it to you. The Family Fun Flight for Four gets you 4 ride tickets and 2 photos for $60.

What: The Roller Coaster at New York New York

Where: New York New York, 3790 Las Vegas Boulevard South

When: Sun-Thur 11 am-11 pm, Fri-Sat 10:30 am-midnight

What's cool about it: Slightly safer than a New York City cab ride.

Gold & Silver Pawn Shop

The guys at the Gold & Silver Pawn Shop have been TV stars since 2009. The family-owned Las Vegas pawn shop is the setting of the hit History Channel reality show "Pawn Stars," and the buying and selling antics of the owners are seen by million of viewers each week.

Fans of the show will want to grab their chance to see the shop in person. There's no guarantee that you'll be able to see the guys from the show, but you might luck into seeing Rick, Corey, Chumlee or The Old Man. You can always try to pawn that Revolutionary War sword that's been gathering dust in your closet. That'll probably lure someone out of the back room.

Even if you don't see an employee you recognize, you'll get a chance to browse the familiar setting of the show. Many of the actual items you've seen them purchase on TV are right there in the store.

A chunk of the store is devoted to Pawn Stars merchandise. Souvenir t-shirts are big sellers. So is pretty much anything with Chumlee's face on it.

The popularity of the television show has vastly increased the popularity of Gold & Silver Pawn Shop. It's not uncommon for visitors to wait in a short line before being admitted, especially during the hours that cast members are most likely to be present (Monday - Friday, 9 am – 3 pm). If you have something to pawn you can walk right in.

Here's one word of warning. If you're not a fan of the show, then Gold & Silver Pawn Shop is simply that –

a pawn shop. You might find something cool you want to buy, but there's nothing particularly glitzy or Vegas-y about it.

You'll find it at 713 Las Vegas Blvd S, about a mile north of the Stratosphere.

What: Gold & Silver Pawn Shop

Where: 713 Las Vegas Blvd. South

When: 9 am-9 pm, daily

What's cool about it: As seen on TV. It's not like drinking in the bar on "Cheers", but it's got 50% more Chumlee.

Dig This

At some point in each of our lives, a grim reality takes hold. We are too old to play in a sandbox. Ed Mumm, the founder of Dig This, disagrees. His super sized sandbox is the perfect playground for adults who want to experience the power of operating heavy equipment.

Who hasn't imagined what it would be like to operate a 10 ton bulldozer or a 15 ton excavator? Aside from construction professionals, and drunken miscreants who break into dig sites after hours, this type of opportunity has not been available to the general public. Thanks to the folks at Dig This, we can all enjoy the experience of operating giant orange machines, but without the annoying jail stay and community service that used to come with it.

The most popular package is the "Big Dig," which includes a pickup from your hotel. After a short bit of safety instruction, you are issued a hard hat and a reflective orange vest, and then it's time to hop aboard your machine. There's only room for one person inside the machine, but don't worry, you'll be in 2-way communication with your instructor through the provided headset. He'll give you a step by step walkthrough of how to work the controls. In a few minutes, you'll be digging and moving heavy objects like a pro.

The entire experience takes about three hours, and includes a large amount of time in the machine. Tasks such as lifting giant tires, digging trenches, moving boulders, and playing excavator "basketball" are provided for your enjoyment. The climate controlled cabs and the ultra friendly staff make the time pass like nothing.

You need to be at least 14 years old and 48 inches tall to operate the machines, but a driver's license is not required. Yes, at Dig This, a 14 year old kid can operate a full-sized bulldozer long before he is licensed to drive.

The Big Dig will cost you $400. A 1.5 hour Mini Dig is available for $210, but a larger percentage of your time is tied up in safety and instruction, so it's not nearly as good a deal.

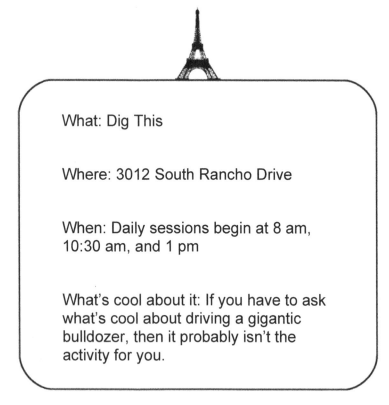

What: Dig This

Where: 3012 South Rancho Drive

When: Daily sessions begin at 8 am, 10:30 am, and 1 pm

What's cool about it: If you have to ask what's cool about driving a gigantic bulldozer, then it probably isn't the activity for you.

Rent an Awesome Car

Seeing the sights in Las Vegas can be fun, but sometimes it's more exciting to be seen. If you're looking to be the center of attention, you can grab a piece of the Vegas spotlight by showing up at your destination in an insanely hot road machine.

Getting dressed up and taking your spouse for an anniversary dinner and a show is nice. Arriving in a limousine is nicer. Pulling up to the front door of a luxury hotel in a Lamborghini Gallardo is the slam dunk champion. You'll have onlookers staring at you, racking their brains to figure out which movie they've seen you in. If you think this seems a little bit excessive, you're wrong. It's a lot excessive. That's the point.

How about a bachelor party with guys piled into a giant Hummer? Or a girls night out in a 1959 Cadillac? There are probably worse ways you can spend your evening than rolling down Las Vegas Boulevard in a Porsche 996 convertible. You're in Las Vegas to have fun. Use your imagination.

There are plenty of places renting luxury cars in Vegas. Here are a few:

Dream Car Rentals www.dreamcarrentals.com
Las Vegas Exotic Rentals www.vegasexoticrentals.com
Beverly Hills Rent-A-Car www.bhlasvegas.com

The cost of the high end stuff is going to sting a bit. Expect to pay upwards of $500/day for a Ferrari or $1000/day for a Lamborghini. Some of the rental companies will ease the pain by renting their most expensive models by the half-day.

Even if you aren't going whole hog car crazy, you might like the sound of a Jaguar at $79/day when you compare it to that subcompact Suzuki you were about to rent. It pays to shop around, because the deals are out there.

One thing all of these companies have in common is their demand for insurance. You'd better have some. It seems that they're under the impression that you might do something crazy in one of their cars... like drive it in Las Vegas.

Neon Museum

Las Vegas changes quickly. Over the years, there has been an ongoing push to replace the old with the new. Buildings get imploded and new, shinier buildings get erected in their places. Many of the new attractions are spectacular, but there's a sadness that comes with losing bits of the city's past. That's why it's so encouraging to see what the folks at the Neon Museum have done.

At the Neon Museum, their mission is to preserve the cool neon signs that are such a large part of Las Vegas history. The signs are collected in an outdoor "boneyard," and can be viewed as part of a guided tour. The tour guides have great knowledge and enthusiasm about old Vegas. As they help you navigate through the two acres and 150+ signs in the boneyard, they're sure to fill your head with facts about the signs, the people who made them, and the properties that displayed them.

The Neon Museum is also dedicated to restoring historic lighted signs and displaying them in places where they can be appreciated by all. Many classic signs, like the horse and rider from the Hacienda Hotel, or the magic lamp from the old Aladdin Hotel, are located around the perimeter of the Fremont Street Experience. Other restored signs, like the giant slipper from the Silver Slipper Casino, light up Las Vegas Boulevard, between The Strip and downtown.

The museum isn't open for general admission. You can't just walk into the boneyard and look around.

Tours are available by appointment. It is best to book your tour at least 1-2 weeks in advance at their website, neonmuseum.org, as they often fill up. The tour costs a $15 donation, which is tax deductable (they give you a receipt).

The tour take place entirely outdoors, and there is no shade to speak of, so be prepared to spend 60-90 minutes in the Las Vegas weather. Wear a hat. Bring sunscreen. Closed-toe shoes are recommended. They'll let you bring a bottle of water, so do it.

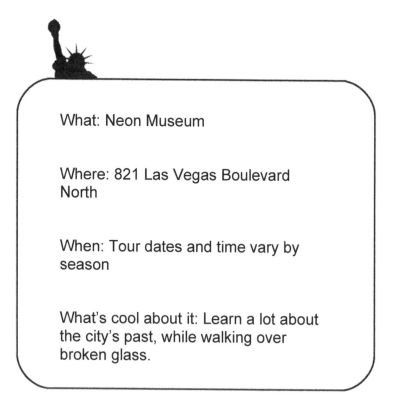

What: Neon Museum

Where: 821 Las Vegas Boulevard North

When: Tour dates and time vary by season

What's cool about it: Learn a lot about the city's past, while walking over broken glass.

Zero G

Las Vegas is a city that built its own Statue of Liberty and Eiffel Tower. It features majestic fountains and water shows in the middle of the desert. Does it come as any surprise that visitors have the option to ignore gravity?

The Zero G company flies a specially modified Boeing 727 jet out of Las Vegas' McCarron Airport a few times a year. By flying a series of high-altitude parabolic arcs, they can create periods of weightlessness for adventure tourists who are up to the challenge. This isn't that little lightness you feel in your stomach when you go over a peak on a roller coaster. This is real, astronaut-type floating in midair (or mid-plane).

After an orientation video and a safety demonstration, you're off to the fly zone. The first parabola simulates Martian gravity (about one third of Earth gravity). The second parabola simulates gravity on the moon (one sixth of Earth gravity). Each successive parabola provides about 30 seconds of outer-space-type weightlessness. You can do flips, bounce off the walls or walk on the ceiling. Whatever feels right. Figure on 7-8 minutes of weightlessness on the approximately 90 minute trip. After you land, there's a Regravitation Celebration, where they hand out photograph souvenirs and your completion certificate. Refreshments are served, in case you need to replace anything you barfed up during your journey.

It's all very cool, and the price is steep. At $4,950 per head, it's no wonder that many of the Zero G testimonials come from celebrities. Las Vegas icons Penn and Teller did it. So did astronaut Buzz Aldrin and household guru Martha Stewart. Physics god Stephen Hawking had a blast on his flight.

The flight schedule varies each year. You'll want to check them out at gozerog.com, so you can make a reservation plan your trip to coincide with a flight date.

What: Zero G

Where: McCarran International Airport

When: Flight dates vary, for the latest, check gozerog.com

What's cool about it: It's the fastest weight loss plan known to man, though it is temporary.

Shark Reef

What's the last thing you expect to see in the middle of the Nevada desert?

If you answered "sharks," then you would be incorrect.

Since the Shark Reef Aquarium opened in Mandalay Bay in 2000, over ten million visitors have witnessed sharks in the desert. Shark Reef is the only predator-based aquarium and exhibit in North America, housing 15 different species of sharks and over 2000 creatures in all.

The largest tank is a 1.3 million gallon monster, designed to resemble a sunken shipwreck. You can walk through an acrylic tunnel as the sharks and other wildlife pass to your left, to your right and above your head. Some of the sharks are as much as nine feet long, and you're pretty darn close to them.

If you crave more than sharks, don't worry. The other exhibits have no shortage of exotic and dangerous creatures. The various tanks include angelfish, puffer fish, piranha, and a selection of nasty venomous fishes. The impressive reptile selection includes a giant green sea turtle, a rare golden crocodile, and an immense komodo dragon.

Also popular is the 2500 gallon saltwater touch pool, where you can actually reach in and touch stingrays, eels and horseshoe crabs. A naturalist is present at all times to make sure visitors and creatures behave.

This is not a sideshow exhibit. Shark Reef is the only facility in Nevada to be accredited by the Association of Zoos and Aquariums. Education is the large part of the experience. Visitors are given audio listening wands which explain the various exhibits in a variety of languages. Educational tours are available twice a day, consisting of a one-hour tour and a one-hour classroom session (which is perhaps more education than the average Vegas visitor is signing up for). Guided tours are also available by appointment. Dive certified guests of Mandalay Bay also have the opportunity to SCUBA dive in the shipwreck tank by participating in the Dive with Sharks Program.

Shark Reef is open seven days a week. Adult admission is $18.00, children 5-12 cost $12.00, and kids 4 and under are free. The Dive with Sharks Program costs $650 for one diver, and a slightly more reasonable $1000 for two divers.

What: Shark Reef

Where: Mandalay Bay Resort and Casino, 3950 Las Vegas Boulevard South

When: Sun-Thur 10 am-8 pm, Fri-Sat 10 am-10 pm

What's cool about it: It's like Shark Week on the Discovery Channel every day!

Circus Circus / Adventuredome

The Circus Circus hotel and casino is one of the oldest in Las Vegas. Underneath the big circus tent and the enormous neon clown, it's also one of the few remaining kid-friendly stops in town. Underneath the big top is a carnival midway, featuring an extensive video arcade and a large selection of carnival games. It's like a miniature version of your state fair, only it isn't that miniature. It's an opportunity for kids to pay a few bucks, play a game, and maybe win a cool prize, which isn't a whole lot different from what the adults are doing downstairs in the casino.

The circus theme is supported by a procession of world class circus acts. Acrobats, aerialists and trapeze artists perform daily, beginning at 11 AM. A schedule is posted, and it's worth stopping what you're doing to watch.

Also on the property is Adventuredome, which bills itself as the largest indoor theme park in the U.S.. The "indoor" part is very important, especially if you plan on visiting during the summer months. The MGM Grand had an outdoor amusement park that closed in 2000, due in part to broiled tourists.

Adventuredome is absolutely loaded with rides and activities. There's the Canyon Blaster roller coaster, with two loops, two corkscrews, and speeds of up to 55 mph. The Slingshot tosses you into the air and drops you, delivering 4 g's of acceleration joy. If your tastes are less adventurous, there's a nice selection of family rides and junior rides.

You can get soaked on a water ride, play laser tag, bungee jump, climb a rock wall, and still have time for 18 holes of miniature golf. There are also a couple of "4D rides." One features Spongebob Squarepants and the other stars Dora the Explorer. These are basically 3D movies with motion simulator seats. Free clown shows run during the afternoons (and into the evening on Fridays and Saturdays).

Most activities are priced individually, but your best deal is an all-day pass ($26.95, or $16.95 if you're less than 48" tall).

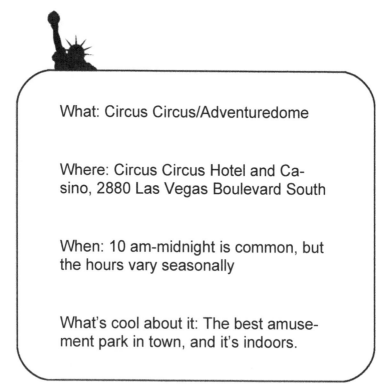

What: Circus Circus/Adventuredome

Where: Circus Circus Hotel and Casino, 2880 Las Vegas Boulevard South

When: 10 am-midnight is common, but the hours vary seasonally

What's cool about it: The best amusement park in town, and it's indoors.

Special Events

Las Vegas has a seemingly limitless capacity to house and feed visitors. That makes it an ideal location for a wide variety of special events. Check your schedule and plan your trip to coincide with one of these attractions.

NASCAR Racing

Once each year, NASCAR comes to the Las Vegas Motor Speedway. The exact weekend will vary, but you get a Nationwide Series race on Saturday and a Sprint Cup Series (the major leagues) race on Sunday. It's a blast to see the drivers and their teams all around town. The weekend is scheduled during the spring, so you're less likely to get broiled in the Vegas sun.

Holidays

New Year's Eve and the Fourth of July are huge events in Vegas, with plenty of fireworks and fun. Halloween and St. Patrick's Day are big, because the city is always looking for an excuse for a party. Memorial Day and Labor Day are always huge events, because everyone loves a three day weekend.

Super Bowl Sunday

Super Bowl Sunday is the unofficial national holiday. In Las Vegas, there are huge viewing parties everywhere. Nevada is the only state that allows legal betting on NFL games, and thousands of people come to town to place their Super Bowl bets. There's nothing like watching the big game in a room filled with people who have bet thousands on the outcome.

World Series of Poker

The World Series of Poker is a series of poker tournaments that culminates in The Main Event, a No Limit Texas Hold 'Em extravaganza that pays a grand prize of over $8 million to the winner. The tournaments usually begin in late May and run into the middle of July. During the Main Event, the town fills up with players, spectators and partiers. A good selection of celebrity players also show up for the Main Event.

National Finals Rodeo

The National Finals Rodeo is the premier championship rodeo event in the U.S. It comes to Las Vegas each year, for ten days in the early part of December. The town fills up with real, authentic cowboys and cowgirls, and the various music venues offer big name country music acts. Even if you have zero interest in the rodeo, it could be worth a trip just to see a few concerts.

Concerts

Speaking of concerts, Las Vegas has hundreds to choose from each year. Is your favorite musical act on tour, but skipping your hometown? They're probably not skipping Las Vegas. Venues like The House of Blues (at Mandalay Bay), The Joint (at Hard Rock Hotel and

Casino), and The Pearl (at The Palms) host some big acts in relatively intimate settings.

Boxing

If it's a huge, important boxing match, there's a pretty good chance it's going to take place somewhere in Las Vegas. There's nothing like a championship fight night in Vegas. Celebrities come pouring in, and the entire atmosphere of the town gets cranked up to an even crazier than usual level. Plenty of venues are capable of hosting fights, but the MGM Grand is the current king of the big fight.

Mixed Martial Arts

Ultimate Fighting Championship (UFC) is the big dog in the world of mixed martial arts, and its popularity is growing fast. UFC is based in Las Vegas, and you can count on them to schedule a handful of fight cards here each year. A UFC fight night is almost as big a deal as a championship boxing fight night, and the various afterparties fill the local clubs with athletes and celebrities.

Conventions

In 2010, over 18,000 conventions were hosted in Las Vegas. The city hosted 60 of the 250 largest trade shows in North America, and 6 of the top 10. The Consumer Electronics Show hosts over 120,000 techies each January. Pack Expo is for people in the packaging industry. REcon is for real estate professionals. No matter what you do for a living, there's probably a convention in Las Vegas for people in your chosen field. If you're looking for an excuse to make your next Las Vegas trip, all it takes is a little planning to make that combination work/play convention happen.

Mystère

"Mystère" was the first Las Vegas-resident show from the acclaimed Canadian troupe Cirque du Soleil. It premiered at Treasure Island in 1993, and over 8000 performances later it is still going strong. Six additional Cirque shows have popped up on The Strip, but with one possible exception, the first remains the best.

What is "Mystère"? If you walk around Treasure Island, you might see a video teaser for the show that uses the phrase, "Words don't do it justice." They're right. Some have called it a circus without animals. Others have called it performance art. Nothing quite fits. You can describe the various pieces of the show without managing to describe the show.

The pieces are impressive. World class-acrobats, colorful costumes, exquisite makeup, innovative world-beat music, skilled aerialists, ingenuous choreography, clowns who are actually funny, and two ridiculously strong and well-balanced brothers, come together in a unique showroom designed and built especially to house the production.

The various ingredients create an atmosphere that is dreamlike. Surreal. A very pleasant sensory overload. If you focus too intently on one performance, you might miss something that's happening in a far corner of the stage, or even in the aisle next to your seat.

The 1600 seat showroom sells out frequently. Purchasing tickets in advance is strongly advised. Seats range from $76 - $120. If you've never paid that much for a show, this is a good place to start. Without giving away too much, let's just say that the entertainment starts before the scheduled show time. It's a good idea to be in your seat at least 20 minutes before the curtain goes up.

What: Mystère

Where: Treasure Island, 3300 Las Vegas Boulevard South

When: Sat-Wed 7 pm, 9:30 pm

What's cool about it: It's like nothing you've ever seen, unless you've seen another Cirque show. And even then, it's pretty darn good.

Terry Fator

When Terry Fator appeared on the second season of America's Got Talent, he thought it might help his career. After all, the ventriloquist from season one had parlayed the exposure into an appearance on the Late Show with David Letterman. Fator was hoping to do the same.

He got his wish and quite a bit more. He won the America's Got Talent title, which led to a deal to perform in Las Vegas. After some successful months at the Las Vegas Hilton, he signed a five-year contract to headline at The Mirage for a reported $100 million. As Fator is fond of saying, it took him 32 years to become an overnight sensation.

What's so sensational about Fator? He's a ventriloquist who understands something that a lot of guys in his business forget. It isn't enough to make the puppet talk without moving your lips. The puppet has to have something to say; preferably something funny.

When the puppets aren't being funny, they sing, and it's the singing that elevates Fator from entertaining to amazing. If you close your eyes, it's easy to believe you're hearing Etta James performing "At Last," but you aren't. It's some white guy holding a puppet. And that isn't his only trick. His vocal range borders on the freakish. He can go from Lynard Skynard to Elvis Presley to Marvin Gaye to Kermit the Frog to Guns 'n' Roses to Sonny and Cher to Gnarls Barkley to Garth Brooks in a single performance. Plenty of vocalists with less talent have made an excellent living in Las Vegas, and they were moving their lips!

Tickets to see Terry Fator range from $65 to $150. As for adult content, it tops out at PG, so it's okay to bring the kids (as long as they are age 5 or older).

What: Terry Fator

Where: The Mirage, 3400 Las Vegas Boulevard South

When: Tue-Sat 7:30 pm

What's cool about it: Dude sounds like a lady. Or a heavy metal singer. Or pretty much anyone.

Celine Dion

Celine Dion grew up as the youngest of 14 children. If she ever lacked attention as a child, her phenomenal popularity as a performer has more than made up for the deficit. Her original show at Caesars Palace, "A New Day," ran for five years from 2003-2007 and spanned 717 performances, most of them sellouts of the over 4000-seat Colosseum. She returned to Caesars in 2011 to begin another three-year engagement.

Her current Caesars show is a slightly more modest offering than the lavishly produced "A New Day," but it's hardly a bargain basement effort. Dion performs on a six-segment modular stage and is backed by a 31-piece orchestra and band, but the show is mostly about her voice. That's enough to carry any show.

Fans will still get to hear her biggest hits, but she has added an eclectic mix of songs by other stars to her performance. Without giving away too many details, let's just say you'll get to hear her take on favorites from Stevie Wonder, Ella Fitzgerald, Billy Joel, Paul McCartney and Wings, and Michael Jackson.

There's another large difference between this run and her original engagement, and that is the frequency of performances. Dion performed "A New Day" over 140 times a year, but she is currently planning to only 70 shows per year. For instance, her 2011 slate has no shows scheduled between August 14 and December 28. If seeing Dion is the main reason for your trip to Las Vegas, then be sure to check the Caesars Palace box office online first.

The prices of tickets to see Celine Dion vary widely, from $95 to $250. Many Vegas shows have VIP packages, but Caesars doesn't stop at just one. There are Ruby, Emerald and Diamond packages available online right now, and who's to say there won't be more by the time you read this. Visit caesarspalace.com to choose the combination of dinner/drinks/souvenirs/seating you would like in your VIP package.

What: Celine Dion

Where: Caesars Palace, 3570 Las Vegas Boulevard South

When: 7:30 pm, dates vary widely

What's cool about it: A huge star in her prime.

Absinthe

The "Absinthe" production show has been described as a mix of Cirque du Soleil and "The Rocky Horror Picture Show." That might not be the best way to explain this mix of burlesque, circus acts and vaudevillian comedy, but it gives you sufficient warning that you are about to witness something highly unusual.

The show is designed for an adult audience. You will hear sexual innuendo and language as vile as language gets, and you'll also get to look at a few attractive women wearing pasties. If this sort of thing offends you, then you will be offended. Don't think you can "tough it out." The humor of The Gazillionaire (the ringleader) and Penny (his oddly appealing assistant) pulls no punches.

If very adult language doesn't both you, you're likely to find it hilarious. The humorous banter and audience participation bits are lighthearted interludes between the more serious performances. There's a dash of cabaret-style singing and dancing, along with various acts of strength, balance, and acrobatics in the style made famous by Cirque du Soleil.

"Absinthe" is performed on a small, circular stage, and the audience sits close. Very close. Before one act, The Gazillionaire warns people in the front row to stay seated, "or you might get kicked in the ****ing head." If you end up in the back row, you're still not more than fifty or sixty feet from the performance.

The show takes place in a large tent in front of Caesars Palace. The temperature in the tent is climate controlled, but the wait to get seated leaves you out in the elements. Seating is general admission, so you need to arrive early if you plan to sit in a particular place, or have a group that wants to sit together. VIP tickets are also available, giving the holders access to a private pre-show bar, and the first crack at getting seated.

Regular seats are $69 and the VIP option will cost you $99. "Absinthe" had a very successful 7-month run in 2011, and was extended for an unknown length of time. You should be OK for most of 2012, but check the Caesars website to make sure it's still there.

What: Absinthe

Where: Caesars Palace, 3570 Las Vegas Boulevard South

When: Wed, Sun 8 pm, Tue, Thur, Fri, Sat 8 pm and 10 pm

What's cool about it: Uninhibited fun inside a big tent.

Elton John: The Million Dollar Piano

Elton John's original Caesars Palace residency show, "The Red Piano," was scheduled to run for three years and 75 performances. The audience's demand for the still-spry Sir Elton led to a two-year extension and 241 shows from 2004 - 2009. Even that wasn't enough for his huge legion of fans.

In 2011, John began a new three-year residency at The Colosseum at Caesars Palace. This time, the piano is no longer red. The show is called "The Million Dollar Piano," named after the extraordinary instrument it took Yamaha four years to custom craft.

Over the course of a nearly two hour performance, John visits most of the high points of his illustrious 40-year career. "Benny and the Jets," "Rocket Man," and "Goodbye Yellow Brick Road" are just a few highlights from the massive hit list. He also takes time for some of the more obscure album cuts that have special meaning to him.

You're likely to hear Elton make the occasional quip about his new, large instrument, and it is quite impressive. The Million Dollar Piano is equipped with 68 state of the art LED screens, capable of displaying anything from an accompanying light show to full-blown video. The piano also sounds great, but that has a lot to do with the man playing it.

John's love of performing has not diminished over the years. In spite of his very busy schedule, he can still be counted upon to produce a show worthy of his very lofty name.

Elton John still tours all over the world, so you have to plan carefully if you want to catch his "Million Dollar Piano" show. Dates are released in batches on the Caesars Palace website, usually a few months before the shows. Ticket prices range widely, from $55 to $250 per seat.

What: Elton John: The Million Dollar Piano

Where: Caesars Palace, 3570 Las Vegas Boulevard South

When: 7:30 pm, dates vary widely

What's cool about it: It's an opportunity to gather and admire Sir Elton's enormous instrument

Penn and Teller

There are plenty of magic and illusion shows in Vegas, but none of them can match the show that Penn and Teller put on. You've probably seen them on television. Penn is the big, loud guy who talks almost constantly. Teller is small, smiling guy who never speaks at all. They have been amusing and amazing audiences at the Rio since 2001. They perform all of their tricks as part of the Rio show before they do them anywhere else, so even if you've seen them elsewhere (another city, on TV, etc...), there will be some new stuff to enjoy.

Here's what you can expect if you go. Penn is going to talk. A lot. Every trick has a story, and Penn is there to tell you the story. Penn is smart, obnoxious, irreverent and funny. Very funny. If you like grim, dark humor, you're going to like Penn.

The tricks are clever, often resembling the illusions of other popular magicians, but with a macabre Penn and Teller twist. Many of the tricks feature the impending puncturing, mutilation or outright death of one of the two stars (usually Teller), but everything turns out all right in the end.

Penn and Teller are known for breaking the cardinal rule of magicians by showing the audience how the tricks are done. You'll definitely pick up a few behind the scenes tidbits about how magic is done, but with these guys nothing is ever as it seems. The explanation can leave you more baffled than the original trick.

Part of the show is interactive, so you could get the enjoyable/terrifying experience of joining the duo onstage. Don't worry, though. Their billboards and bus signs around town brag of "Fewer audience injuries than last year!" So you should be just fine.

Penn and Teller perform six nights a week (not on Friday) at the Rio hotel/casino, just west of The Strip. Tickets run $75-$95. They hang out in the lobby after most every show, posing for pictures, signing autographs, and just hanging with the audience. That's pretty nice.

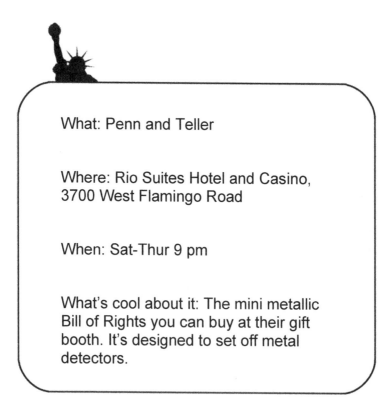

What: Penn and Teller

Where: Rio Suites Hotel and Casino, 3700 West Flamingo Road

When: Sat-Thur 9 pm

What's cool about it: The mini metallic Bill of Rights you can buy at their gift booth. It's designed to set off metal detectors.

O

Cirque du Soleil's "O" (a play on words with the French word for water, eau) opened at the Bellagio in 1998, and is still one of the most popular shows in town. If Cirque's "Mystère" isn't the best production show in Las Vegas, then "O" takes the prize.

The similarities to "Mystère" are significant. The showroom was custom built for this show, so the sightlines are excellent. The music, costumes and sets create a moody, dreamlike atmosphere. The acrobatics and dancing are world class. The clowns inject comic relief at regular intervals. And there is often more happening on stage than your eyes can track at one time.

The biggest difference is the water. The eau. The O. There's one and a half million gallons of it in the performance pool, and it opens up new possibilities in artistry and athleticism. Synchronized swimming is made possible. Aerialists can now dismount from high in the air, twisting and spinning their way towards graceful splash landings. Audience members can get water on their best go-to-the-show clothes (though only in the first couple of rows, and not all that much water, really).

When is a pool not a pool? When it's covered by an awesome retractable stage. The "O" stage can function as a normal show stage, retract fully to allow access to the pool, or retract partially, giving the impression that the performers are walking on water. The producers use the flexibility in clever and entertaining ways.

"O" is frequently honored as the best production show in town, so you're going to have to pay for quality. Tickets range from $93.50 to $150.00. If you have the choice between being close or sitting a little farther back in a center section, choose the center.

What: O, by Cirque du Soleil

Where: Bellagio, 3600 Las Vegas Boulevard South

When: Wed-Sun 7:30 pm and 10 pm

What's cool about it: Don't underestimate the feat of making synchronized swimming tolerable.

Jabbawockeez

Showgirls aren't the only dancers you can find in Las Vegas. Since 2010, the Monte Carlo has been the home of the Jabbawockeez dance troupe, the former champions of "America's Best Dance Crew."

The members draw upon their hip hop and B-Boy cultural background to tell stories using music, dance and humor. (Don't know what a B-Boy is? Think "breakdancer," and you won't be far wrong, though nobody uses the term "breakdancer" anymore.)

The crew dresses in identical white masks and gloves, a move designed to keep attention focused on the group, as opposed to an individual dancer. The impression left is that of a group of synchronized mimes, with outrageous talent and incredible moves. Since the masked dancers do not speak, the music is the most important thing you will hear. To the relief of some and the disappointment of others, this is not a 90-minute hip hop show. The style is hip-hop, but the musical content is varied. During various segments, you'll hear the songs of Prince, Michael Jackson, Coldplay, Beyoncé and Queen.

Las Vegas does not offer a large selection of shows that are family-friendly, but this is one of them. The target audience is probably in the age range of 10-30, but you'll see a variety of folks, up to and including senior citizens, enjoying the show. The dancers frequently interact with audience members in the closer rows, but there's nothing that you or your kids would be uncomfortable doing.

The Jabbawockeez crew performs at the Monte Carlo each Thursday through Monday. Tickets range from $62-$95. A lot happens on stage, and you probably don't want to be closer than row 10 if you want a good view of it all.

What: Jabbawockeez

Where: Monte Carlo Resort & Casino, 3770 Las Vegas Boulevard South

When: Sun-Tue 7:30 pm, Thurs-Fri 9:30 pm, Sat 7 pm and 9:30 pm

What's cool about it: Breakdancing is still cool in 90-minute doses.

Brad Garrett's Comedy Club

You probably remember Brad Garrett as the towering, deep-voiced Robert from "Everybody Loves Raymond". Garrett is also a hilarious standup comedian. In 2010, he took over the Comedy Stop at the Tropicana and turned it into Brad Garrett's Comedy Club. As part of the deal, the new club is the only place in Las Vegas where you can see Garrett perform.

The first thing Comedy Stop veterans will notice is the dramatic improvement in décor. The room is clean and fresh. The old chandelier has been shined up. Classy red curtains and a zingy piano player give the place some old Vegas charm.

Garrett himself doesn't perform every night. He schedules himself for a handful of weekends a year, and there's always a small chance that he'll show up unannounced. Most evenings feature other comedians, and the quality is quite high. Garrett is a veteran of the comedy circuit, and he knows who is funny and who isn't.

Here's a tip worth trying. Take a look at their schedule and see which comedians are performing when you are in town. Bip on over to You Tube and look up the comedians in question. You can usually find a couple of representative clips that'll give you an idea of what you're getting into. Even if you pick a random night to attend, you're likely to get two funny performers.

When Garrett himself is in town, the show is a must see. He has headlined at some of the largest venues in town, so if you want to see him in the more intimate club setting, you should book early.

Tickets are $39 for regular seats or $59 for VIP seats. The VIP seats give you a closer view, but also increase your chance of becoming a target of the more interactive performers.

*** Last second update – Literally hours before press time, Garrett announced that he is moving his club to the MGM Grand in March 2012. Expect the same high-quality performers, and of course, frequent standup shows by Garrett himself.

What: Brad Garrett's Comedy Club

Where: Tropicana Las Vegas Hotel & Casino, 3801 Las Vegas Blvd. South

When: Sun-Thur 8 pm,
Fri-Sat 8 pm and 10 pm

What's cool about it: Cutting edge comedians from a man who knows the standup comedy world.

KÀ

The Cirque du Soleil productions residing in Las Vegas can be categorized this way: three acrobatic shows ("Mystere," "O," "KÀ"), two musical shows ("Love," "Viva Elvis"), one sexy show ("Zumanity") and one magic show ("Criss Angel Believe"). "KÀ" is the third Cirque show featured in this book, and it's no coincidence that all three are of the acrobatic variety. That's where Cirque got its start, and it's still what they do best.

From the moment you enter, the KÀ Theater gives off an ominous vibe. Lighted platforms line the walls to the right and left of the audience. Painted tribesmen appear on the platforms; a few at first, but progressively more as show time approaches. In the place where you might expect to see a stage, there isn't one. All you can see is a smoking, glowing orange pit.

The stage becomes visible when the show begins, and quickly becomes one of the stars of the show. It is a massive contraption comprised of two platforms, and weighs in at over 80 tons. It is maneuvered by a combination of cranes and hydraulics that allow the "terrain" to change between or even during scenes. It can transform from a traditional flat surface to various degrees of incline, or even a sheer, vertical wall. Different acrobatic feats are made possible by each variation.

"KÀ" differs from other Cirque offerings by telling a linear story. The action centers on a pair of twins who are separated and must overcome obstacles to become reunited. It's not an innovative or complex story, but it provides a thread that connects the various action sequences.

Those action sequences are excellent and often spectacular. The costumes, makeup and sets are extraordinary, but for Cirque, extraordinary has become the norm. No show has ever sounded better. Every single seat has a pair of speakers at ear level, and there are hundreds of additional speakers in various parts of the theater.

"KÀ" is the resident show at the MGM Grand. Tickets range from $75 to $165 for adults. Children 5-12 are half price.

What: KÀ

Where: MGM Grand Hotel & Casino, 3799 Las Vegas Boulevard South

When: Tue-Sat 7 pm and 9:30 pm

What's cool about it: Acrobatics on stage, and a stage that does acrobatics

The Amazing Jonathan

You might be familiar with The Amazing Jonathan from his Comedy Central specials or his many appearances on Late Night with David Letterman. "The Freddie Krueger of Comedy and Magic" has been headlining in Las Vegas since 2001, and his current home is Planet Hollywood.

Jonathan differs from the standard Las Vegas magician in some important ways. He doesn't wear a tuxedo, preferring to dress in a style you might call "psychotic casual." Then there's a small problem with his magic. It stinks. It's not good. Most of his tricks fail, or don't even manage to reach a climax. Don't worry, though. That's not just part of the act. It is the act. The magic is just the method he uses to deliver his warped comedy. The Amazing Jonathan isn't really there to amaze you; he's there to make you laugh.

If you like your comedy dark, this is your guy. His gags are grim and twisted. If you like your comedians filthy, he's still your guy. It's definitely a no kids zone.

Jonathan is aided by his assistant, Psychic Tanya. Psychic Tanya is blonde and clueless. She is the ruiner of tricks and the butt of jokes. You get the feeling that if Jonathan ever actually managed to saw her in half, she might not notice.

Audience participation is a big part of the show, at least for one person. During every performance one audience member is brought up on stage to assist with some tricks. If you end up being the lucky victim, then wave goodbye to your date. You're going to be on stage for upwards of half the show. But look on the bright side. You'll have an emotionally scarring story to tell for the rest of your life.

A ticket will run you $65. If you sit close to the stage, you risk ending up on the stage. Keep that in mind.

What: The Amazing Jonathan

Where: Planet Hollywood, 3667 Las Vegas Boulevard

When: Tue-Sat 9 pm

What's cool about it: Can't do a card trick to save your life? There still might be a career for you in Las Vegas.

Barry Manilow

Barry Manilow has sold over 80 million records in his illustrious career. If you own even one of them, you'll want to take the opportunity to see Manilow live at Paris Las Vegas. For Manilow's most rabid fans (his Fanilows), the guy could perform in a dark alley and that would be fine with them. The rest of us demand a bit of class, and Barry's Paris show more than delivers. World class lighting and high-definition video screens provide some striking visuals. A crew of talented backup singers and a majestic orchestra help with the music.

And the music is what it's all about. Manilow has reached a point that most musicians can barely imagine. He has more top 40 hits than he can possibly fit in a 90-minute show. We are talking about literally dozens of hits from every decade reaching back to the 1970s. Sure, you'll probably hear "Mandy" and "Could it be Magic" and "Copacabana," but there just isn't enough time to play them all.

Barry is getting up there in years (born in 1943), so he can't hit every note the way he could when he was a kid. Still, his voice is astonishing and his showmanship has always been top notch.

If you're planning a Vegas trip, don't just assume Manilow will be performing while you're in town. He performs about 6-12 shows a month, mostly on week-ends. It's worth checking an online schedule, and it never hurts to buy tickets in advance.

Ticket prices vary widely from $95 to $299. If you want to see Barry up close it's going to cost you, but the 1500-seat showroom is intimate enough that you really won't feel deprived if you end up sitting near the back of the room.

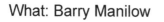

What: Barry Manilow

Where: Paris Las Vegas, 3655 Las Vegas Boulevard South

When: 8 pm, dates vary widely

What's cool about it: Barry doesn't do those big world tours anymore, so Vegas is your best chance to see him.

Jubilee!

If you're looking for a bit of old school Vegas entertainment, you owe it to yourself to take in the Jubilee! show at Bally's. Jubilee! completed its 30th year in 2011, making it the longest-running production show in town. It is the last show in town to feature the archetypical Las Vegas showgirls, and it has survived this long by being the best.

The show kicks off with the song "Hundreds of Girls." A quick count will tell you that there aren't a hundred girls, but they aren't too far off. You can see immediately that the girls are the real thing. Actual authentic Las Vegas showgirls. They are elegant and statuesque, with towering headdresses that weigh as much as 35 pounds and costumes you could fit into a teacup.

The program alternates between large, lavish production numbers and smaller, quieter specialty acts. You might get a big song and dance number, followed by a juggler, then another song and dance, followed by a pair of contortionists. The specialty acts serve the double purpose of being entertaining in their own right, and also allowing the showgirls a few minutes for a costume change. Those minutes are important, since over 1000 costumes are used in the show.

The scale is grand. The stage is enormous. The sets are huge, from the toppling temple in the Samson and Delilah number to the sinking of the Titanic.

In the tradition of old Las Vegas, most of the showgirls are topless. The nudity is presented so tastefully that you almost don't notice it. Almost. For those who would rather not attend a topless show, the early (7:30 p.m.) Saturday show has the "coverage" you desire.

Tickets range from $57.50 to $117.50. Admission is adults only, except for the early Saturday show which allows kids as young as 13 with a parent or guardian.

What: Jubilee!

Where: Bally's Las Vegas, 3645 Las Vegas Boulevard South

When: Sat-Thur 7:30 and 10:30

What's cool about it: It's the last bastion of good, old fashioned nakedness on The Strip.

Donny and Marie

The musical pairing of siblings Donny and Marie Osmond goes all the way back to 1973, when they performed together at Caesar's Palace in Las Vegas. A few decades and a hop across the street later, you can find the duo headlining at the Flamingo.

She's still a little bit country and he's still a little bit rock and roll, and the old stage chemistry remains. Viewers of their 1970's era variety show will remember that one of the show's signatures was the comedic banter between brother and sister. There's still plenty of it. After all of these years it's obvious that they continue to enjoy performing together.

They can still get around, too. While the show is backed by a team of dancers, the stars can still show some footwork when they have to. It was just 2007 when Marie finished third on Dancing with the Stars. Donny won the competition in 2009.

Their rapport with the audience is impressive to behold. Fans don't just love the show; they can't get enough of it. The number of repeat visits is very high. People see the show again and again. In response to that, Donny and Marie did a major revamp of their playlist in 2011.

The 90-minute show contains numerous duets, but also features solo opportunities for each singer. Donny brings a new version of "Yo Yo," the 1971 hit that brought him fame when he was fronting The Osmonds. Marie responds with a Glee-style mashup of Aerosmith's

"Walk this Way" and Nancy Sinatra's "These Boots Were Made for Walkin'."

Tickets range from $95 to $125 for regular seats. If you want the full Donny and Marie experience, a $260 VIP ticket gets you front-of-stage seating and a photo with the stars after the show.

What: Donny and Marie

Where: Flamingo Las Vegas, 3555 Las Vegas Boulevard South

When: Tue-Sat 7:30 pm

What's cool about it: the 20-story-tall building wrap of D&M on the outside of The Flamingo.

Human Nature

The next time you go to Las Vegas, here's what you should do. Go to the Imperial Palace. Sit in a 650-seat showroom. Watch and listen as four white guys from Australia sing a selection of great Motown songs. If this sounds like a strange bit of advice to you, that's perfectly normal. There's nothing about that description that makes the Human Nature show sound particularly compelling, especially in the competitive environment of Las Vegas entertainment. The full name of the show gives a clue that there might be something more here. It's called "Smokey Robinson presents Human Nature: The Ultimate Celebration of the Motown Sound".

Hmm. If Smokey likes them, that's got to mean something. Right?

Absolutely. The guys come out sharp, with matching suits and ties, and shoes so shiny you'll squint when the stage lights hit 'em. Their high-energy combination of song and dance is like taking a time capsule back to the golden era of Motown. Their range is considerable. They can do the Jackson 5 one minute and Marvin Gaye the next. Even when they tackle songs from female artists like the Supremes, it still works.

The quartet is backed by an excellent six-piece band, but it's their amazing voices that carry the show. The a cappella numbers are some of the most impressive.

Tickets to Human Nature can range from $54.95 to $76.95. Since the showroom is relatively small, it's a good idea to purchase them in advance if you don't want to risk disappointment.

These guys are good. Really good. Don't be surprised if they're in a bigger and better venue by the time you visit. Check them out online at their website, humannaturelasvegas.com to make sure you're going to the right place.

What: Human Nature

Where: Imperial Palace, 3535 Las Vegas Boulevard South

When: Sat-Wed 7:30 pm

What's cool about it: Australian dudes singing Motown. Crikey!

Mac King Comedy Magic Show

The Mac King Comedy Magic Show is a Las Vegas oddity for two reasons. First, it's a daytime show. King does a 1:00 PM show and a 3:00 PM show and that's it. He goes home to his family.

Second, it's the extremely rare type of show that manages to entertain all audiences. Children and grannies. Bikers and accountants. Everyone loves it. King even claims to get the occasional smile from surly teens, but he might be exaggerating.

It is what it claims to be; a comedy and magic show. King has a folksy kind of charm. He begins each show with a wave and a "howdy." He is naturally funny and easy to like. He has the standard stage magician toolbox of card tricks, rope tricks, goldfish tricks, and... Fig Newton tricks? His sleight of hand is among the best you will find anywhere.

Audience participation is a large part of the show, as audience members are frequently chosen to help out with the tricks. If the thought of being singled out by a Las Vegas comedian terrifies you, then put your mind at ease. King isn't going to make fun of your weight or your wife or your toupee. He's not that kind of guy. Kids are frequently chosen to play the role of assistant, because it's all harmless fun.

A good daytime show is like magically finding extra time in your vacation. You get to see a good show in the afternoon, and you still have the whole night in front of you. King's show is perennially voted the best daytime show in town.

The Mac King Comedy Magic show happens on Tuesday through Saturday at Harrah's Hotel and Casino, and it's a heck of a deal. You can pay the full $32.95 admission price and count it as one of the best show deals in town. Or you can be a little proactive and find yourself a coupon. Harrah's frequently hands out good coupons for the show, either just inside or just outside their main entrance.

What: Mac King Comedy Magic Show

Where: Harrah's Las Vegas, 3475 Las Vegas Boulevard South

When: Tue-Sat 1 pm and 3 pm

What's cool about it: Finally, something better to do with Fig Newtons than eating them.

Phantom – The Las Vegas Spectacular

There's always some trepidation when a popular Broadway show gets "Vegasized." More often than not, the Broadway to Las Vegas transition leaves us with a pale, weak imitation of the original. Thankfully, that's not the case with the revamped version of "Phantom" that resides at The Venetian.

There are a few reasons for the excellent result, but none are more important than the involvement of Andrew Lloyd Weber and original "Phantom of the Opera" director Hal Prince. With the guidance of Weber and Prince, the show was shortened to a Vegas-friendly 95 minutes. Only the intermission and some transitional scenes were cut. The storyline and every one of Weber's songs remain. Longtime "Phantom" fans approve of the slimmed down production.

The Venetian invested $40 million in a custom-built Phantom theater, and the result is dazzling. The design is intended to replicate the luxury of the Paris Opera House. The walls are lined with opera boxes inhabited by dozens of mannequin "patrons." Each mannequin is uniquely designed and posed, and all are outfitted in authentic period dress. No expense was spared in the creation of the iconic Phantom chandelier. The four-tiered, $4.5 million crystal creation is sure to grab your attention. Let's leave it at that.

None of the technical details would matter if the players could not hold up their end of the bargain. Not to worry. The Broadway-caliber cast comes through nicely. This version of the show is dense with song, but the voices of Anthony Crivello (Phantom) and Kristi Holden (Christine) are strong enough to carry the day.

Ticket prices vary from $59 all the way up to $250 for the VIP package. The VIP deal gets you a backstage tour, a meet and greet with the cast, and gold circle orchestra seating.

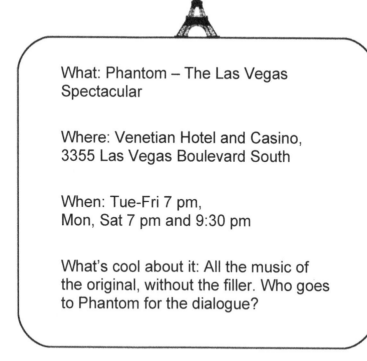

What: Phantom – The Las Vegas Spectacular

Where: Venetian Hotel and Casino, 3355 Las Vegas Boulevard South

When: Tue-Fri 7 pm,
Mon, Sat 7 pm and 9:30 pm

What's cool about it: All the music of the original, without the filler. Who goes to Phantom for the dialogue?

Blue Man Group

How do you describe the Blue Man Group show at The Venetian? Some have called it performance art. Some have called it mime (how's that for a four letter word?). Some have called it random acts of weirdness. One thing is for sure, you won't find anything else in Vegas quite like it.

It starts with three men dressed all in black, only their hands and their bald heads are uncovered. Those body parts are covered with a thick, shiny layer of blue greasepaint. The result is three men who look almost exactly identical and just a bit creepy.

Once arrived, these alien creatures engage in what can broadly be described as antics. Some props include paint, Jell-o, Twinkies, marshmallows, and a couple of miles (really!) of rolled paper. Some of it is smooshed. Some of it is squirted. Some of it is hurled across the stage and caught in a Blue Man's mouth. It's clever. It's funny. It's very lighthearted. It's also very loud, so be prepared.

Even though none of the Blue Men speak, music and sound are a large part of the show. Cap'n Crunch is used as a percussion instrument. PVC plumbing pipes are played as drums. A good sized band, comprised of non-blue men and women, backs up the trio with an upbeat, rock soundtrack played on both traditional and unusual instruments.

Audience participation is a part of every show, so if you don't want to end up on stage, think twice before sitting in the first few rows. Also, those close up seats are referred to as the "Poncho Section." If you sit in one of these seats, you receive a poncho to protect you from flying... stuff.

Ticket prices range from $74.90 to $147.50. Internet discounts are often available to selected shows at blueman.com.

What: Blue Man Group

Where: Venetian Hotel and Casino, 3355 Las Vegas Boulevard South

When: 7 pm and 10 pm, daily

What's cool about it: Holy crap! What isn't cool about them?

Jersey Boys

Jersey Boys is the story of Frankie Valli and the Four Season; four young guys from (you guessed it) New Jersey. This musical tells the rags-to-riches story of four boys from Newark who become one of the most successful pop groups of all time. The show premiered on Broadway in 2005, and has won enough Tony, Grammy, and other awards to fill a very sizable trophy case.

The Las Vegas edition of the show came to the Palazzo in 2008, and it does the Broadway version proud. Many Broadway productions are truncated for Las Vegas, but this one weighs in at a stout two hours and ten minutes, with a brief intermission.

The story of the band members and their 40-year friendship is punctuated by energetic renditions of the group's many hits. Some high points are "Sherry," "Big Girls Don't Cry," "Oh What a Night," "Can't Take My Eyes Off of You". The dramatic performances are excellent, and the musical pieces have audiences standing and clapping.

The show is always one of the most popular in town, so your best bet is to purchase tickets in advance. Seats will run you $73 - $161. If you want the VIP treatment, with front and center seating, your own private entrance (that allows you to view Four Seasons and Rock and Roll Hall of Fame memorabilia), and a souvenir program, that'll cost you $260 per seat.

The show warns that it contains "strong authentic Jersey language and is not appropriate for all ages." That means a good handful of f-bombs during the dramatic portions of the show, so be prepared. Children ages 5 and under are not allowed. For kids older than that, it's up to you to decide if they're ready to hear Jersey-style street talk.

What: Jersey Boys

Where: The Palazzo, 3327 Las Vegas Boulevard South

When: Tue, Sat 6:30 pm and 9:30 pm, Sun, Wed-Fri 7 pm

What's cool about it: Men with incredibly high voices, yet somehow still manly.

Garth Brooks

Part of Steve Wynn's goal at his Las Vegas properties is to "give people something they can't get anywhere else." In this case, that means Garth Brooks. When Wynn coaxed Brooks out of an eight-year retirement to perform at the Encore Hotel, it was a pretty simple deal. Garth gets anything he wants. Aside from an undisclosed amount of cash, which, when stacked, is probably taller than the Stratosphere tower, and a private jet to take him to and from his home in Oklahoma, this is what Garth wants. He wants an intimate feel to his show, with no over-the-top production and pyrotechnics. He wants to walk out on stage in jeans, cowboy boots and a baseball cap, sit down on a stool, and play his acoustic guitar.

Once on stage, he spends a good bit of time talking to the audience. It almost feels like you went over to a friend's house for the evening, and he just decided to pull out the guitar on a whim. He talks about his many musical influences, and plays a bit by each of them. There is no set playlist, but you're likely to hear songs from any or all of Bob Seger, Simon and Garfunkel, George Jones, Merle Haggard, Billy Joel or Jim Croce. During most shows he will be joined on the stage by his wife, Trisha Yearwood, and they will sing a couple of duets together. On top of all that, there's still time to hear a fistful of Garth's hits. The 90-minute Vegas show standard doesn't apply here, as the performance frequently creeps past two hours.

If you want to see Garth in Vegas you have to plan carefully. His five-year engagement at the Encore is scheduled to last until 2014. Brooks does four shows per weekend, but only 15 weekends a year. Almost all of the shows are on Fridays or Saturdays. You need to check the dates at wynnlasvegas.com.

A ticket will cost you about $250. You can (and should) order tickets in advance, but all tickets must be picked up in person at the will-call window at the resort. Tickets are non-transferrable and not scalpable.

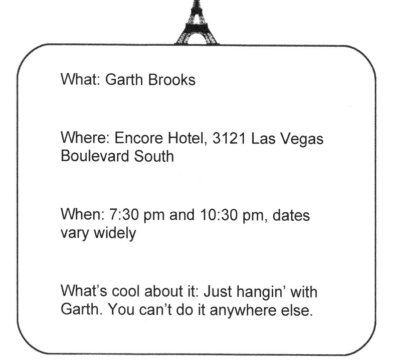

What: Garth Brooks

Where: Encore Hotel, 3121 Las Vegas Boulevard South

When: 7:30 pm and 10:30 pm, dates vary widely

What's cool about it: Just hangin' with Garth. You can't do it anywhere else.

Le Rêve

"Le Rêve" (French for "the dream") is the brainchild of Franco Dragone, the creator of the two most popular Cirque du Soleil shows, "Mystère" and "O". Like other Dragone shows, there is some attempt at telling a story, but you're not likely to assemble the various pieces into any kind of cohesive narrative. It's a dream. It's weird. It's not supposed to make perfect sense.

Fortunately, it doesn't have to make sense to be highly entertaining. Like Dragone's Cirque shows, "Le Rêve" features a large cast of skilled gymnasts, dancers, aerialists, divers and swimmers whose performances can deliver anything from great beauty to jaw-dropping athleticism.

The technical design of the production is impressive. The 1600 seat theater was created especially for "Le Rêve". It is theater in the round, with a 1.1 million gallon pool in the middle. This innovative design allows for a very intimate entertainment experience where no seat is located more than 42 feet from the stage and the closest seat is just 4 feet away. Yeah, if you sit that close you're going to get wet. Sometimes quite wet. That leads to the unusual circumstance of the front row seats being the cheapest seats.

How do the swimmers breathe when their heads are underwater for so long? You can find out if your purchase a dream seating package. This package gets you a nice seat with plenty of leg room and a video monitor. The monitor allows you to see behind the scenes stuff that is not visible from your seat. It lets you watch the goings on both before and during the show. If that's not enough luxury, you can opt for the Champagne Circle seating, which gives you everything in the dream package plus a bottle of champagne, some chocolate-dipped strawberries and a selection of yummy truffles.

"Le Rêve" plays on Friday through Tuesday, twice a night at the Wynn Las Vegas resort. Tickets are $99 for splash zone seats, $129 for regular seats, $155 for dream seating or $195 for the champagne treatment. Children under age 5 are not allowed.

What: Le Rêve

Where: Wynn Las Vegas, 3131 Las Vegas Boulevard South

When: Fri-Tue 7 pm and 9:30 pm

What's cool about it: A little water won't kill you. Watch the show from only four feet away.

Tix 4 Tonight

Tix 4 Tonight isn't entertainment (unless ticket shopping is a hobby of yours), but it does allow you to save money on your Las Vegas entertainment purchases. Each morning at 9:30 AM they release a big batch of discounted Vegas show tickets for public purchase. All you have to do is browse through their offering, pay a couple of bucks in service charge, and purchase show tickets at 20-50% off of the box office price.

Actually you're purchasing a voucher that can be redeemed at the box office of the show in question. Not to worry, though. Tix has been around for a few years, and they (and their vouchers) are totally legit.

It's a phenomenal deal, but it does have some limitations. Most of each day's available tickets are for that night's shows, so there isn't much of a chance for advance planning. You also have to purchase your voucher at one of their locations (nine on The Strip, and a couple of others). They don't do phone or internet sales. Their website will give you a sneak preview of some of the shows available, but you have to show up in person to see the full, extensive list.

Showing up in person has another benefit. Most of their locations have brochures for the various shows, so you can research the various offering before you make a choice.

An old criticism of Tix goes something like this: "They've got discounted tickets, but not to any of the good shows." There might have been some truth to that statement a few years ago, but not any longer. Their daily inventory is larger than ever. Tickets to many of the shows featured in this book can often be found at a nice discount. If you've got your mind set on a specific show, you results with Tix will be hit or miss, but if you're flexible, the place is a gold mine.

They have recently branched into food coupons. For $2-3 per coupon, you can save money at a variety of Las Vegas restaurants and buffets.

What: Tix 4 Tonight

Where: A dozen locations on The Strip and downtown

When: Hours vary by location, 9 am-9 pm is common, but opening and closing times can vary by an hour

What's cool about it: Saving bunches of cash is always cool.

Index

Absinthe, 179
Adventuredome, 167
aquarium, 71, 90, 165
Aria, 32, 120
Atomic Testing Museum, 107
Aureole, 43
Bellagio, 25, 27, 31, 33, 53, 65, 67, 73, 84, 112, 120, 129, 130, 151, 185
Bellagio Fountain Show, 25, 27, 53, 65, 73, 84
Bellagio Gallery of Fine Art, 129
Blue Man Group, 99, 207
Bodies... The Exhibition, 145
Bonanza Gifts, 95
Border Grill, 45
Brad Garrett's Comedy Club, 189
Brooks, Garth, 175, 211
buffets, 33, 216
Burger Bar, 41
Caesars Palace, 8, 19, 21, 89, 119, 134, 152, 177, 179, 181
Carnegie Deli, 17
Carnival Court, 55

CBS Television City Research Center, 137
Cheesecake Factory, 8, 59, 60, 90
Circo, 27
Circus Circus, 167
Cirque du Soleil, 27, 173, 179, 185, 191, 213
Consumer Electronics Show, 171
Cosmopolitan, 34, 112
CSI The Experience, 121
day spas, 119
Delmonico Steakhouse, 61
Desert Pines, 105
Dig This, 157
Dion, Celine, 65, 177
Donny and Marie, 199
Encore, 111, 135, 211
Excalibur, 35
Exotics Racing, 139
Fashion Show Mall, 93
Fast Lap Indoor Kart Racing, 125
Fator, Terry, 175
Feniger, Susan, 45
Firefly, 51
Flamingo, 81, 133, 199

Forum Shops, 8, 19, 21, 89
Four Queens, 11
Fremont Street Experience, 97, 161
GameWorks, 115
Gold & Silver Pawn Shop, 155
Golden Nugget, 134
golf courses, 105
Grand Canal Shoppes, 91, 131
Grand Canyon tour, 127
Grand Lux Café, 59
Hard Rock Hotel, 135, 170
Hash House a Go Go, 57
helicopter tours, 127
House of Blues, 170
Human Nature, 201
Imperial Palace, 58, 101, 201
Jabbawockeez, 187
Jean Philippe Patisserie, 31
Jersey Boys, 209
Joël Robuchon, 47
John, Elton, 181
Jubilee!, 197
KÀ, 191
Keller, Hubert, 41
Lagasse, Emeril, 49, 61
Las Vegas Motor Speedway, 139, 169
Lavo, 63
Le Cirque, 27
Le Rêve, 213

Luxor, 77, 113, 145
M Resort, 34, 58
M&M's World, 115
Mac King Comedy Magic Show, 203
Madame Tussauds, 99
Mandalay Bay, 39, 42, 44, 88, 120, 133, 165, 170
Manilow, Barry, 195
Marquee, 112
Max Brenner, 19, 90
MGM Grand, 47, 49, 77, 85, 115, 121, 134, 167, 171, 192
Milliken, Mary Sue, 45
Mirage, 15, 17, 71, 73, 105, 107, 141, 175
Mon Ami Gabi, 53
Monte Carlo, 187
Mystère, 173, 185, 213
N9ne Steakhouse, 37
NASCAR, 115, 169
National Finals Rodeo, 170
Neon Museum, 161
New York New York, 77, 83, 152, 153, 154
Nightclubs, 111
Overton, David, 59
Paiute Golf Resort, 106
Palazzo, 60, 74, 92, 209
Palmer, Charlie, 43
Palms, 38, 112, 135, 171
Paris Las Vegas, 53, 83, 130, 195
Pawn Stars, 155
Penn and Teller, 164, 183

Phantom – The Las
  Vegas Spectacular, 101,
  205
Picasso, 25, 129
Pinball Hall of Fame, 123
Planet Hollywood, 21, 34,
  147, 193
pools, 82, 111, 120, 133,
  134, 135, 165, 185, 213
Qua Baths and Spa, 119
Rain, 112
Red Square, 39
Rio, 23, 69, 183
roller coasters, 77, 152,
  153, 154, 163, 167
Samba Brazilian
  Steakhouse, 15
Secret Garden and
  Dolphin Habitat, 141
Serrano, Julian, 25
Shadow Creek, 105
Shark Reef, 165
Show in the Sky, 69
Showcase Mall, 115
Sirens of TI, 75
special events, 169
Spice Market Buffet, 34
Stratosphere, 13, 127,
  144, 149, 156, 211
Stratosphere Thrill Rides,
  149
Stripper 101, 147
Studio B Buffet, 34
Sushi Roku, 21, 90
Tao, 111
The Amazing Jonathan,
  193

The Auto Collections, 101
The Bank, 112
the bathhouse, 120
The Gun Store, 117
The Joint, 170
The Pearl, 171
The Price is Right – Live,
  109
Titanic The Artifact
  Exhibition, 113
Tix 4 Tonight, 116, 215
Top of the World, 13
TPC Las Vegas, 106
Treasure Island, 75, 173
Tropicana, 123, 189
Vegas Indoor Skydiving,
  103
Venetian, 60, 62, 74, 91,
  99, 111, 131, 152, 205,
  207
volcano, 8, 73, 107
weddings, 151
Welcome to Las Vegas
  Sign, 87
Wicked Spoon Buffet, 34
Wine Cellar and Tasting
  Room, 23
World of Coca Cola, 115
World Series of Poker,
  170
Wynn Las Vegas, 33, 119,
  214
XS, 111
Zero G, 163

Also from MYOL Books

Which casino games are beatable?

How much should I tip the dealer, valet, or cab driver?

How do I get a free hotel room?

Win more!   Spend less!
Navigate Vegas like a pro!

Lightning Source UK Ltd.
Milton Keynes UK
UKOW06f2330141215

264698UK00009B/379/P